MEDIAEVAL CHURCH VAULTING

AMS PRESS

NEW YORK

MEDIAEVAL CHURCH VAULTING

BY

CLARENCE WARD

ASSOCIATE PROFESSOR OF ARCHITECTURE, RUTGERS COLLEGE
LECTURER ON ARCHITECTURE, PRINCETON UNIVERSITY

PRINCETON UNIVERSITY PRESS
PRINCETON
LONDON: HUMPHREY MILFORD
OXFORD UNIVERSITY PRESS
1915

Library of Congress Cataloging in Publication Data

Ward, Clarence, 1884–
  Mediaeval church vaulting.

  Original ed. issued as no. 5 of Princeton monographs in
art and archaeology.
  Bibliography: p.
  1. Vaults (Architecture) 2. Church architecture.
3. Architecture, Medieval. I. Title. II. Series:
Princeton monographs in art and archaeology, 5.
NA5453.W3 1973   726'.59   72-177847
ISBN 0-404-06836-7

Trim size of original copy was 7 1/2 X 10 1/4. This
edition has been reduced to 6 X 9. Text size has also
been reduced by 5%.

Reprinted from an original copy in the collections of the
Newark Public Library.

From the edition of 1915, Princeton
First AMS edition published in 1973
Manufactured in the United States of America

AMS PRESS INC.
NEW YORK, N. Y.   10003

To A. M.

WITH THE LASTING AFFECTION OF THE AUTHOR,
WHO IS INDEBTED TO HIM FOR MUCH INSPIRATION

INTRODUCTION

The student of Mediaeval architecture, especially of the Gothic era, finds perhaps its strongest appeal in the peculiar structural character which it possesses. Greek architecture, even at its best, strongly reflects a preceding art of building in wood. Roman architecture, when it does not closely follow its Greek prototype, often depends upon a mere revetment or surface treatment for its effects, and the Renaissance builders in general followed this lead. Only in the Middle Ages was the structure truly allowed to furnish its own decoration, and the decoration itself made structural. And by far the greatest single problem of construction was that of vaulting. A knowledge of vaulting is, therefore, essential for the thorough student of Mediaeval architecture. On the vaulting system depend in a large measure the shape of piers and buttresses, the size and form of windows and arches, and a host of decorative mouldings and details which form the complex whole of Mediaeval construction.

Inheriting from Early Christian times a church of well-established plan, the builders of the eleventh to the sixteenth centuries set themselves the problem of substituting for the wooden roof of this Early Christian Basilica a covering of masonry which would resist the conflagrations that were among the most destructive forces of the Middle Ages. It is with these efforts that the following pages are to deal. It has been my purpose to classify and to discuss in a systematic manner what has been gathered from authorities here and abroad and from a study of the monuments themselves.

Especial emphasis has been laid upon the connection between the vaulting and lighting problem. Some vaults, such as those of six-part and five-part form, are shown to have probably derived this form from the clerestory, while other vaults of nave, apse, and ambulatory are proved to be very closely related to the position of the windows beneath them. In the discussion of Romanesque vaulting, a number of churches are suggested as forming a "School of the Loire," in addition to the schools which are generally listed. Suggestions are made regarding the form of the centering employed in Perigord, and there is a somewhat extended account of the purpose served by the triforia of Auvergne. In dealing with ribbed vaults the use of caryatid figures for the support of the ribs, the non-essential character of the wall rib, the origin and development of six-part vaulting, and the types of chevet vaults are subjects especially treated. But these and other novelties are all subordinate to the real purpose of the work, which is to give in a compact and systematic form a thorough résumé of all the principal forms of vaulting employed in the middle ages. For the sake of this systematic treatment the different portions of the church, nave and aisles, choir and transepts, apse and ambulatory have been taken up in separate chapters, though in each case there has been an effort to keep as closely as possible to the chronological sequence of the monuments. This matter of chronology has, in fact, led to an effort to date as accurately as possible all the buildings mentioned. For this purpose the author has consulted many authorities and in the case of doubtful monuments has arrived at the dates given only after an analysis of the various claims advanced.

The illustrations are in large measure from photographs taken by the author or purchased in Europe. The following, however, are from publications, Figs. 31, 34 and 39 from Gurlitt, *Baukunst in Frankreich* (J. Bleyl Nacht, Dresden); Fig. 12 from Baum, *Romanische Baukunst in Frankreich* (Julius Hoffmann, Stuttgart); Fig. 38, from Bond, *Gothic Architecture in England* (Batsford, London), and Fig. 63 from Moore, *The Mediaeval Church Architecture of England* (Macmillan, New York). The drawings are largely based upon plates in Dehio and Von Bezold, *Kirchliche Baukunst des Abendlandes* (Cotta, Stuttgart), supplemented by the author's own notes. Of course, only a limited number of illustrations were possible and for this reason less well known examples, and those not previously published, were in most cases chosen. To make it possible for the reader to supplement the illustrative material references are made in the footnotes to publications in which reproductions of many of the churches mentioned may be found. The books chosen for reference have, where possible, been those easily accessible to the student.

The principal literary sources for the work are listed in the bibliography, though many works not mentioned were also consulted. Among the sources which proved most useful are the works of Choisy, Enlart, Lasteyrie, Rivoira, Porter and Moore, all of which are especially recommended to the student of vaulting. For personal assistance in the preparation and subsequent reading of the work, the author is much indebted to Professor Howard Crosby Butler and Professor Frank Jewett Mather, Jr., of Princeton University, but especially to Professor Allan Marquand of Princeton, under whose inspiration and encouragement the work was undertaken.

CLARENCE WARD.

New Brunswick, New Jersey.
October, 1915.

CONTENTS

CHAPTER I

NAVE AND AISLE VAULTS

During the Romanesque period, or roughly speaking, from the beginning of the eleventh to the middle of the twelfth century, three chief forms of vaulting were employed over the naves and aisles of church edifices. The first of these was the dome, the second the tunnel vault, and the third, groined vaulting. With the development of the ribbed vault, all three gave way to this new method of construction, and the Gothic era was inaugurated.

DOMES ON SPHERICAL PENDENTIVES

The dome was employed in two rather distinct ways according to the form of pendentives used for its support. Thus a number of churches continue the tradition of the spherical pendentive, while in others some form of squinch or trumpet arch is found. Both methods are of early origin, dating back, in fact, to the Roman era preceding the reign of Justinian (483-565) and consequently earlier than the Byzantine architecture of which they are so conspicuous a feature. Rivoira[1] has shown the existence of numerous spherical pendentives of the second century A.D. or even earlier, and Lasteyrie[2] has added to these a small cupola at Beurey-Beauguay (Côte-d'Or) in France dating from the second or third century. But even if this method were known at an early date it was not until the Byzantine era that it obtained a wide-spread and extensive usage. During the sixth century it became the principal method of vaulting throughout the Roman Empire, and, as such, had a considerable influence upon Carolingian architecture of the ninth and tenth centuries. This is true even in France, for traces of pendentives were found in 1870 during a restoration

[1] Rivoira I, p. 29, et seq.; also Lasteyrie, p. 272, et seq.
[2] Lasteyrie, p. 274, and Fig. 268.

I

of the church of Germigny-des-Prés,[3] a fact of particular interest because it is in France that the principal Romanesque examples of this method are to be seen.

DOMES ON SQUINCHES

As for the squinch, it may possibly be of Persian origin, but the earliest examples thus far known in Persia are to be found in the palaces of Firouz Abad and Sarvistan, which probably date from the Sassanian period between A.D. 226 and 641, and are therefore of later date than the Roman examples of the first and second centuries to be found in the Palace of the Caesars at Rome and the Villa Adriana at Tivoli (cir. A.D. 138). Whatever its origin, the squinch in its various forms, simple cross lintel,[4] cross arch, trumpet arch, niche head, etc., was employed prior to and during the Byzantine period along with the spherical pendentive. In fact a trumpet arch of domed up character is found in the Baptistery of the cathedral of Naples[5] which dates from the fifth century, while the niche head or half dome type, very commonly employed in Romanesque architecture, has a sixth century prototype in the church of San Vitale at Ravenna,[6] as well as many earlier examples such as those in the Domus Augustana (cir. A.D. 83),[7] or the Thermae of Caracalla (212-216)[8] at Rome. Other types of squinches occasionally appear but they are generally referable to one of the above mentioned forms.

THE SCHOOL OF PERIGORD

By far the most important group of Romanesque churches employing the dome on spherical pendentives, is situated in that portion of France extending around the city of Perigueux, and constitutes what is known as the architectural school of Perigord. Since Perigueux was a trading post on the route from Venice to the west, it must have felt a good deal of Byzantine influence, and it is the general theory that to this influence is due the almost universal employment of the dome on pendentives in the churches of this school. While this may well be the case, it is nevertheless to be remarked that the dome as a method of vaulting seems to have been

[3] Lasteyrie, p. 270.
[4] Early ex., Umm es-Zeitun illustrated in Rivoira, I, p. 35, Fig. 51.
[5] Rivoira, I, p. 193, Fig. 273.
[6] Rivoira, I, p. 57, Fig. 82.
[7] Rivoira, I, p. 33, Fig. 46.
[8] Rivoira, I, p. 35, Fig. 50.

the only importation, its construction in Perigord differing in almost every particular from that of the Byzantine period. This might even seem to indicate that the Perigord type of dome was not imported, but actually indigenous to this part of France, a theory which has lately been advanced by no less an authority than Lasteyrie.[9] But in any case, the points of difference in construction between the domes of Byzantine architecture and those of the school of Perigord are of more importance in this discussion of vaulting, than is the question of their origin.

COMPARISON OF PERIGORD AND BYZANTINE DOMES

These differences have been so admirably summed up by Lasteyrie[10] that a translation of his summary with a few additions will perhaps give the best possible account of them. They are grouped under six chief heads which may all be studied by using the cathedral of Saint Front at Périgueux (Figs. 1 and 2) as a model. First, the French pendentives are

FIG. 1.—PERIGUEUX, CATHEDRAL.

[9] Lasteyrie, p. 465 et seq.
[10] Lasteyrie, p. 470.

borne on pointed instead of semicircular arches; second, the surface of the pendentive at Saint Front rises from the intrados rather than from the extrados of the voussoirs; third, the diagonal profile of the French pendentive is a complex curve[11] instead of a quarter circle; fourth, the oldest French pendentives have their masonry in horizontal courses while the Byzantine frequently have their courses more or less normal to the curve; fifth the springing of the domes of Saint Front is some distance back from the circle formed by the pendentives, the diameter of the dome being thus greater than its impost,[12] while in Byzantine models, the two correspond; and sixth and last, the domes of Saint Front are slightly pointed and, for that matter, all the French domes are at least semicircular, while the Byzantine domes are generally of segmental section. The explanation of all these differences lies in the material employed, for the domes of Perigord are of stone, those of Byzantine architecture are of brick or some other light material. The pointed arch having less thrust than that of semicircular section was better suited for stone construction, a fact which explains the pointed section of many French domes whose outward thrusts were thereby greatly reduced. Moreover, while the light Byzantine material made possible a dome without centering constructed after the manner of the Egyptian "voute-par-tranches,"[13] the heavy stone of the French ' vault made a centering absolutely necessary, a fact which explains the setting back of the dome from the curve of the pendentives so that the ledge thus formed might serve to support the wooden centering employed.[14] It explains also the horizontal courses since these allowed a greater amount of the weight of each course to be borne by the one beneath it, thus reducing the pressure and making possible a centering of comparative lightness. But these were not the only results of the employment of stone. Since the domes of Perigord are much heavier than the Byzantine domes and exert much more outward thrust it was essential for them to have very firm supports. Perhaps it is with this in view that the churches of this school are for the greater part without side aisles, their outer walls with heavy applied and transverse arches providing suitable support for the domes. Even when aisles exist, they are merely deep wall arches forming trans-

[11] Lasteyrie, p. 472, Fig. 489.
[12] Exception to this at Fontevrault, see Reber, p. 358.
[13] See Choisy, I, p. 20.
[14] See Fig. 4.

verse tunnel vaults rising from the level of the imposts of the transverse arches of the nave and, with them, furnishing the support for the triangular pendentives. This is the arrangement in the cathedral of Saint Front at Périgueux (Fig. 1), the only church in France of this particular type.[15]

The Exterior Roofing of Perigord Domes

One advantage in the employment of the dome of stone lay in the fact that it might be faced on both the exterior and the interior, or covered directly by tiles without the use of a bonnet of wood and copper, or a roof of wood and tile, so frequently seen in Byzantine work. It is doubtful whether the earliest French domes were treated in this way, however, for indications would seem to point to the original employment of a wooden roof over the domes of the cathedral of Saint Front.[16] Nevertheless, these domes have since been restored with an exterior stone facing (Fig. 2), and a similar treatment is to be seen at Cahors cathedral, and over

FIG. 2.—Périgueux, Cathedral.

the crossing of Angoulême. In these domes the drum is first built up in a slightly ramping wall, to offset the outward thrust of the vault, and the dome itself is crowned by a lantern toward which it has an upward curve,

[15] Other examples, all in Cyprus:
1) Peristeroma. 2) Hieroskypos. 3) Saint Barnabas. 4) Larnaca. Enlart, I, p. 210, and p. 286, note 3.
[16] Lasteyrie, pp. 473, 474.

rendering the exterior steep enough to shed water readily. At Angoulême the domes of the nave are entirely concealed by a gable roof, perhaps in the early manner of the school. Still another type of dome covering appears at Saint Étienne in Périgueux,[17] where the curve of the dome does not show on the exterior, but where the drum is first carried up around the haunch, and then surmounted by a flattened conical roof of tile, which rests directly upon the vault beneath.

CHARACTERISTICS OF PERIGORD CHURCHES

It has already been noted that the employment of the dome on pendentives over square bays led to the construction of churches with a broad nave without side aisles. Among the earliest of these are the church of Saint Astier (Dordogne), (founded about 1010 but so mutilated as to show little of its original construction),[18] and Saint Avit-Sénieur (Dordogne) (cir. 1117), originally with three domes which were replaced by domed up Anjou vaults in the thirteenth century.[19] The best of the earlier examples remaining for critical study are, first, the cathedral of Saint Pierre at Angoulême, whose western bay was constructed between 1100-1125,—the remaining three being but slightly later—and second, the church of Saint Étienne at Périgueux, originally with four domes, two of which were destroyed in the religious wars of the sixteenth century. Of the two which remain the more recent must be earlier than 1163, and the other would seem from its appearance to be about contemporary with that of the west bay of Angoulême.[20] These two with the cathedral of Saint Front (after 1120) furnish three excellent examples of the school, to which a large number of other churches might be added as illustrating some minor differences in plan or elevation.[21] The cathedral of Angoulême (Figs. 3 and 4) is characteristic of the school. Deep wall, and heavy transverse arches supply substantial impost for the domes. The piers of the western bay are of simple rectangular plan like those of Saint Avit-Sénieur and Saint

---

[17] Lasteyrie, Figs. 491 and 498. Also cathedral of Cahors (original state) Fig. 495.
[18] See Lasteyrie, p. 473 and Enlart, I, p. 211, note 1.
[19] Lasteyrie, p. 474, Fig. 490.
[20] See Lasteyrie, p. 475.
[21] Among them, Cahors (Lot) Cath. (consecrated 1119); Souillac (Lot) Ch., Plan, Lasteyrie, Fig. 493; Fontevrault (Maine et Loire) Ab. Ch., Plan, Lasteyrie, Fig. 494; Gensac (Charente) Ch. (wooden roof over dome), Plan, Lasteyrie, Fig. 356. Section Lasteyrie, Fig. 496; Solignac (Haute-Vienne) Ch., (consecrated 1143).

Étienne at Périgueux, while those to the east are of a later compound type with transverse arches and wall-arches in two orders instead of the

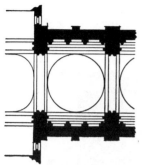

single order of the earlier bay. Except over the crossing, where there is a high circular drum forming a lantern, the domes are not pierced with windows around their base. This is due to the fact that they are covered on the exterior by a wooden roof.[22] It is more usual to find four small windows at the base of each dome as in Périgueux, Saint Front (Fig. 1).[23] The use of stone in the construction

FIG. 3.—ANGOULÊME, CATHEDRAL. of the domes explains the small number of these windows compared to that in Byzantine architecture,[24] since the stability of the vault would be threatened by too many openings. Besides this, the fact that the churches of Perigord have no aisles, properly speaking, permitted sufficient light to enter through windows in the side walls. In fact it seems quite possible that the windows in the domes of the Perigord churches were used to afford resting places for the frame work of the centering even more than for light, a fact which would also seem to be true of the four recesses left in the masonry just above the cornice of the domes of Angoulême cathedral (Fig. 4).

THE CENTERING OF PERIGORD DOMES

In support of this theory it is possible to point out that if long cross beams were used in building these domes, it would be difficult if not impossible to remove them after the dome was finished. If, however, as at Angoulême, small spaces were left in the masonry it would be possible to tilt a beam bevelled at each end and resting on the ledge of the dome and thus remove it without cutting. Still another argument in favor of this theory is the fact that the open spaces to north and south are above the level of the ledge, which would seem to indicate that they were planned to receive the end of a cross beam at right angles to, and above the one running lengthwise. Of course, when windows took the place of these

[22] See also Gensac, Lasteyrie, Fig. 496, and Solignac, Fig. 264.
[23] Also Cahors Cath.,—Périgueux Saint Étienne, etc.
[24] See comparison of Périgueux, Saint Front, and Venice, San Marco in Lasteyrie, p. 470, Fig. 486 and p. 471, Fig. 487.

small recesses the removal of the beam could be made through them. There remain, however, a number of churches in which there are neither windows nor recesses, but in most of these the ledge of the dome is itself wide enough to support a beam which could be removed without striking the vault surface.

FIG. 4.—ANGOULÊME, CATHEDRAL.

As for the choirs of the churches of this school, they were occasionally domed as at Saint Front[25] (Fig. 1), but were more often covered by a tunnel vault terminating in the half dome of the apse. The eastern portion of the choir of Saint Front (Fig. 1) and the choir of Angoulême (Fig. 4) illustrate this latter arrangement.

NAVES VAULTED WITH DOMES ON SQUINCHES

Although very frequently used over the crossing of Romanesque churches, the dome on squinches is seldom found over the bays of the nave.

[25] Also Peristeroma (Cyprus), Enlart, I, p. 210 and p. 286, note 3; Hieroskypos Cyprus), Enlart, I, p. 210 and p. 286.

There is in fact no distinct school in which this method is employed and the examples of its use are widely scattered. The principal one is, perhaps, the cathedral of Notre Dame at Le Puy (Haute-Loire), which dates from the eleventh and twelfth centuries. Unlike the domed churches of Perigord it is of basilical plan with side aisles. The nave is in six bays with broad arches opening into the aisles and a triforium arcade above them. Across the nave are transverse arches separating the bays. The four toward the east are semicircular, the remaining two are pointed in elevation. These arches rise from imposts nearly or quite as low as those of the nave arcade, and walls are built upon them to the level of the string-course above the triforium. Six rectangular bays,—or seven including the crossing,— of practically square plan are thus formed and each is covered with a dome. In the western bays,—which are at least a century later than those at the east end and therefore more advanced in structure,—a clerestory wall is erected with a single window in its north and south walls, and openings corresponding to windows from one bay to the next above the transverse arches, to secure a good distribution of light (Fig. 5). Across the upper corners of these four walls and rising from the same level as the window heads, are arches with half domed triangular niches beneath them, converting the square into an octagon and furnishing the impost for the domes.[26] These are octagonal in elevation as well as plan and are laid up in flat panels, or gores, which meet at the crown (Fig. 6). It is a type of dome admirably suited to its impost since it presents none of the awkward appearances of a circular dome on an octagonal base.[27] It is also very practical from a structural standpoint. Since the gores are flat, the stone cutting is far less elaborate than in a hemispherical dome, and the gored dome has the further advantage of great flexibility since it may be flattened or raised at the crown, placed over a square bay or one with any number of sides, and made equilateral or with gores of different widths, all with great facility. Furthermore, when the naves are of reasonable width, as in most churches with side aisles, the thrust of the dome is very slight and its downward pressure is not excessive.

[26] The clerestory is omitted in the earlier bays and the crossing has peculiar vaulting described in a later chapter.

[27] See Rivoira, I, p. 35, Fig. 51 and Lasteyrie, p. 267, Fig. 259 for examples of this awkward type.

But with all its structural advantages, a system like that at Le Puy was not a satisfactory solution of nave vaulting. The transverse arches were necessarily so far below the surface of the dome that the continuity of the

Fig. 5.—LePuy, Cathedral.

Fig. 6.—LePuy, Cathedral.

nave as a whole was destroyed, and the appearance was rather that of a series of lantern towers or crossings juxtaposed than of a single homogeneous vault.

The side aisles of Le Puy are of less importance than the nave, though the fact that some of their bays were vaulted, or revaulted, at nearly every period of mediaeval architecture makes them interesting for a study of consecutive methods. In the bays to the east the vaults are groined on stilted, round headed transverse arches in the early Romanesque manner, while the succeeding bays have pointed transverse arches with groined vaults closely resembling those of the school of Bourgogne, and the bays nearest the west end have ribbed vaults, in one case with the early heavy-torus rib, in another with the light rib of pointed section of a late Gothic rebuilding.

Although not the basis of a school of Romanesque architecture, the cathedral of Le Puy was not without its influence. This is especially apparent in the large church of Saint Hilaire at Poitiers (Figs. 7, and 8),

FIG. 7.—POITIERS, SAINT HILAIRE.

which was constructed with very broad nave and aisles,—both covered with wooden roofs,—after a disastrous fire of 1018, and dedicated in 1059. In 1130 the vaulting of this church was undertaken, the result being a most unusual edifice. As the nave was too broad to be easily covered by a vault of single span, it was subdivided by lofty and slender piers and arches into a central portion consisting of square bays,[28] and narrow rectangular bays forming veritable inner aisles on either side. These narrow bays were covered with groined vaults directly above the original clerestory windows which thus continued to light the newly formed nave. Domes were then placed over the square central bays as had been done at Le Puy, but instead of the niche-head-squinch and the practically equilateral octagonal dome, small conical trumpet arches were employed at Saint Hilaire, and the gores of the dome rising from these were much narrower than the four remaining panels. This gives the dome rather the character of a cloistered vault with its corners cut off than of a dome properly speaking. Since the clerestory is below the level of the transverse arches upon which the domes of Saint Hilaire are built, the interior has a loftier and less broken appearance than that of Notre Dame-du-Puy. But even so the effect is not remarkably pleasing.

The side aisles of Saint Hilaire (Fig. 8) are quite as interesting in their vaulting as the nave. A single broad aisle on either side, which apparently opened into the nave through lofty arches rising almost to the clerestory, and which probably had transverse arches with ramping walls carrying half gable roofs, was altered when it was determined to vault the church. In doing this, two arches with a solid wall above were placed under each of the original arches of the nave arcade, a slender column built up in the center of each of the original bays, and upon the pseudo-double side aisles thus formed, compound groined vaults were constructed in a manner 'best understood from the photograph (Fig. 8).

Except for those just mentioned there are but few Romanesque churches, —outside of Italy and Sicily,—in which the nave is covered by a series of domes.[29] But because of the powerful Byzantine influence, these latter

[28] See Fig. 7. There is one rectangular bay at the end of the transept aisles and this is covered by an interpenetrating vault at the level of the transverse nave arches.

[29] In France, at Champagne (Ardèche), there is a church vaulted in a manner similar to Le Puy, but it is doubtful whether such a method was the original intention of the builders, since each dome is placed over two rectangular nave bays. Enlart, I, pp. 289-291.

countries contain a large number of churches of semi-Byzantine, semi-Romanesque character, some of which are as late as the thirteenth century.[30] Most of these are so distinctly Byzantine that they do not properly

FIG. 8.—POITIERS, SAINT HILAIRE.

fall within the province of this book, in spite of their late date; but others, like the cathedral of Molfetta,[31] have a vaulting system quite closely allied to the Romanesque.[32] In this particular cathedral, a nave of three square

Plan, Fig. 120. This is, however, a most interesting church for the domes are very segmental in section, are supported upon squinches and have transverse arches through their centers. There is also no clerestory and, in fact, the entire church is of the standard Auvergne type except for the vaults. A reference to the drawings in Baudot and Perrault-Dabot, Vol. V, pl. 27, will show this peculiar system.

[30] Among these may be cited: Venice, San Marco, reconstructed 1052 or 1071, dedicated Dec. 8, 1094, but added to and decorated in the twelfth century and later. Canosa, San Sabino (1101). Trani, Santa Maria Immacolata (twelfth century). Santa Maria dei Martiri (near Trani) (also twelfth century). Molfetta, Cathedral (late twelfth and early thirteenth century). Padua, Sant' Antonio (thirteenth century) Byzantine-Gothic type, numerous Silician churches, etc.

[31] Plan, in Cummings, II, p. 18, Fig. 248. Interior in Michel, I, p. 542, Fig. 273.

[32] Similar churches: Trani, Santa Maria Immacolata, plan in Dehio and von Bezold, I, p. 354. Santa Maria dei Martiri, Ch.

bays is covered by three domes, one on flattened spherical pendentives, the others on niche-head-squinches. Two of them rise from drums and unlike their Byzantine prototypes, they are all of stone.[33] Moreover, the side aisles are covered with half tunnel vaults on full transverse arches, the crown of the vaults together with the nave walls above them acting as admirable buttresses for the domes. A system not quite so logical exists in the aisles of the church of San Sabino at Canosa (1100), where there are full tunnel vaults which do not serve so adequately as buttresses.

Pyramidal Vaults

Although not vaulted with domes, the church of Saint Ours at Loches in France (Indre-et-Loire) (Figs. 9 and 10) has a close connection with

Fig. 9.—Loches, Saint Ours.

such churches as those of Perigord and Notre Dame-du-Puy. This collegiate church was probably constructed a little before 1168, and originally consisted of a nave divided into square bays by transverse arches of pointed

[33] Rarely the case in Byzantine architecture.

elevation and side aisles which have now disappeared. Each nave bay is converted from a square into an octagon by flat triangular pendentives on very small trumpet arches. But instead of domes, the builders of Saint

FIG. 10.—LOCHES, SAINT OURS.

Ours substituted a hollow octagonal pyramid of stone over each bay. Such a system, while presenting the same aesthetic objection as that of Le Puy, had greater structural advantages. The pyramids could be built entirely without centering, and exerted almost no outward thrust, while the stones of which they were constructed could be faced on the exterior (Fig. 9) as well as the interior, and the steep roof thus formed provided adequate drainage for the rain and snow of the region.[34]

TUNNEL VAULTS

If the dome played but a small part in Romanesque architecture, such was not the case with the tunnel vault. Almost as old as civilization itself, this method of vaulting had been employed to a greater or less extent in every age from the Egyptian period to that of the Carolingian Empire. It is natural, therefore, to find it the principal method in use during the entire Romanesque era. Nor is it necessary to trace its history back to Persian or Armenian sources. The builders of the eleventh and subsequent centuries had plenty of examples nearer at hand. Roman vaults, some of them of stone, were still in a good state of preservation in many parts of the western world, and almost every country or province possessed examples dating from Carolingian days.[35] It is not the use of this roofing system, therefore, but the skill with which it was adapted to the naves and aisles of churches of basilical plan, that furnishes the most interesting features in the study of Romanesque tunnel vaulting. In fact, so distinct are the combinations and methods employed in different regions, that they constitute veritable architectural schools which may be classified and separately discussed.[36]

ROMANESQUE SCHOOLS OF TUNNEL VAULTED CHURCHES

The four major schools lie in France and center around the ancient provinces of Provence, Poitou, Auvergne, and Bourgogne, whence they derive their names. All four are comprised in practically the same period, —namely, the eleventh and part, at least, of the twelfth centuries,—and it would be impossible to arrange them in any chronological order. But from its resemblance to the Roman monuments in the midst of which it grew and the fact that it had comparatively little structural influence upon the other schools, Provence will be the first to be considered.

[34] Choisy (Choisy, II, p. 201) thus accounts for the vaults, which would then be variants of Perigord domes, but the plan and supports of the pyramids suggest the influence of Le Puy.

[35] Examples in France: Grenoble, Saint Laurent (crypt of the seventh or eighth century), Germigny, des-Prés (ninth century), etc. Examples in Italy: Milan, Sant' Ambrogio (choir of the ninth century), Agliate, etc.

[36] For illustrations of Romanesque churches and vaults, the reader is advised to consult Lasteyrie, Dehio and von Bezold, and Enlart.

THE SCHOOL OF PROVENCE

The cities of Arles and Nîmes had been important Roman provincial centers. Moreover, they still retained, and to this day possess, a large number of Roman monuments whose influence upon the Romanesque churches of the eleventh and twelfth centuries is plainly apparent. Thus vaults which carry directly the tiles of the roof, single aisled churches resembling the little Nymphaeum, or so-called temple of Diana at Nîmes, the employment of flat pilasters in place of the more usual applied shafts of curved section, and a host of minor details all reflecting classic usage are marked characteristics of this school.

PROVENCE CHURCHES OF THE FIRST TYPE

When considered from the point of view of vaulting, the churches of Provence fall into five distinct groups. The first, illustrated by the chapel of Saint Gabriel near Tarascon (Bouches-du-Rhône),[37] is composed of churches with no side aisles. These are covered with tunnel vaults of semicircular or pointed section, with or without transverse arches and carrying directly the tiles of the roof. The supporting walls are frequently strengthened by a series of interior applied arches in one or more orders thickening the wall at the impost of the vault. Outside of this interior buttressing, which has already been seen in Perigord, the churches of this type are of little structural interest.

PROVENCE CHURCHES OF THE SECOND TYPE

In the remaining groups, side aisles are always present and these have four distinct vaulting systems. In the first, tunnel vaults are employed throughout the edifice. Saint Nazaire[38] (after 1090), the former cathedral of Carcassonne (Aude), though somewhat removed from the center of the school, illustrates this system. Both nave and aisle vaults rise from the same impost level. The vault of the nave is slightly pointed, those of the aisles are semicircular, and both have transverse arches. It is a simple and practical method of construction, since the aisle vaults furnish admirable abutment for that of the nave, and all three are covered by a gable

---

[37] See also Montmajour (Bouches-du-Rhône); Saint Martin-de-Londres (Hérault); Saint Pierre-de-Redes (Hérault); Mollèges (Bouches-du-Rhône), Saint Thomas. See Reber, pp. 337, Figs. 201-202.

[38] Also Lérins (Alpes-Maritimes), Saint Honorat (portion).

roof of masonry resting directly upon the vault crowns. Its one great fault is the absence of direct light in the nave, a condition which introduces the problem of lighting a tunnel-vaulted church.

THE LIGHTING OF TUNNEL-VAULTED CHURCHES

This problem was second only to that of constructing the vaults themselves and, furthermore, it had much to do with the forms which these assumed and even with the plan of the church. When there were no side aisles, windows were cut directly through the outer walls, but to introduce a clerestory above an aisle arcade involved a number of structural difficulties. The side aisle vaults no longer aided in supporting that of the nave, and in fact exerted an inward pressure at a point below its impost where such pressure was most difficult to offset. At the same time, the outward thrust of the central tunnel vault was increased in proportion to its elevation from the ground. The simplest method of meeting these difficulties was to increase the thickness of the clerestory walls, or add simple salient buttresses and trust to good construction to offset the increased thrusts. This was the method adopted by most of the Romanesque builders.[39] It was only in the school of Bourgogne, and under its influence, that the problem received a better solution—which will later be discussed at length—and not until the Transitional and Gothic periods that it was completely solved by dispensing entirely with the tunnel vaults.

While its chief effect was upon vaulting, the lighting problems frequently affected the plan of the church as well. When the nave was without direct light, the aisles were almost always narrowed to permit light to enter from windows in their outer wall. Double aisles were practically impossible,[40] unless the inner aisles had triforium galleries supplied with windows.[41]

Nor did the problem of lighting enter merely into the construction of

---

[39] Early examples: Saint Genou, choir (end of eleventh century), Saint Benoit-sur-Loire, choir (begun 1602), Nevers, Saint Étienne.

[40] The double-aisled abbey church of Souvigny, which has a clerestory, might be cited as an exception to this statement, but judging from the narrowness of its inner aisles (Fig. 19) it would appear as if its nave had originally been deprived of direct light, and that the present clerestory must have been introduced with or without a vault above it, either before or at the time when the outer aisles were added. If so, it would not prove an exception to the rule. The present nave vault is an addition of a late Gothic period.

[41] As in Saint Sernin at Toulouse.

simple tunnel vaulted churches. It was involved with that of all kinds of vaulting throughout the entire Romanesque and Gothic periods. Transverse tunnel vaults like those of Tournus, groined vaults like those of Vezelay, the development of the Gothic chevet from the half domed apse, and the systems of ribbed vaulting which are frequently found in the crossings, aisles, and ambulatories of Gothic churches, all are closely related to the lighting problem.

Provence Churches of the Second Type continued

Returning to Provence, it will be recalled that Saint Nazaire at Carcassonne was described as a typical example of the second class of churches of this school, entirely tunnel vaulted, with narrow side aisles whose lateral windows afford the only light with which the nave is supplied. There are, however, a few churches, vaulted like Saint Nazaire, in which the builders introduced a clerestory. Among these is the abbey church of Saint Guilhem-du-Désert (Hérault) (rebuilt at the end of the eleventh century).[42] Here the clerestory is of considerable height, the heads of the windows lying beneath the imposts of the tunnel vaults, a fact which renders this church one of the most developed of the school. Yet this development lies merely in the presence of the windows, and not in any structural advances which made their presence possible. It was because of the excellent masonry of the heavy walls and piers, that the Provence builders dared to attempt this innovation. The vaults themselves are no lighter than before and still carry the entire weight of the roof. In fact, the whole system is one of inert stability, analogous to Roman construction, and exhibits little if any advance toward the elasticity and balanced thrusts which were to characterize Gothic architecture.

Provence Churches of the Third Type

The churches in the third Provence group differ from those in the second only in having half tunnel vaults in the side aisles, but this difference is sufficient to change to some extent the character and methods of construction. In the simple churches of this type where there is no clerestory as, for example, in the western portion of the little church of Saint Honorat, belonging to the monastery of the Isle-de-Lérins (Alpes-Mari-

---

[42] Reber, p. 341, Fig. 205a, and Lasteyrie, p. 413, Fig. 431.

times),[43] the half tunnel vault of the aisles furnishes better abutment for that of the nave than the full tunnel vaults of the second type, and at the same time permits loftier arches to be constructed in the nave arcades, giving a better distribution of light without raising the imposts of any of the vaults.

When, however, a clerestory is added, as in Saint Trophime at Arles (first half of the twelfth century), the inward pressure of the aisle vaults is even more severe than in Saint Guilhem-du-Désert and at the same awkward place, so that the only structural advantage at Arles lies in the added height of the nave arches. It is a noticeable feature of Saint Trophime that the aisles have full, instead of half arches[44] used transversely beneath the vaults, very probably because the former exerted less inward thrust, and could also be weighed down by a solid wall which increased the rigidity of the structure by tying the pier of the nave arcade to the outer wall, and strengthened the clerestory for the support of the high vault. The system has already been noted in the cathedral of Molfetta,[45] and will be found repeated either in the triforia or aisles of a number of Romanesque churches of different schools.[46]

PROVENCE CHURCHES OF THE FOURTH TYPE

The employment of a three-quarters tunnel vault over the aisles renders the fourth group of Provence churches a cross between the second and third. Like them it contains examples with and without a clerestory. Of these the cathedral at Vaison (Vaucluse)[47] (twelfth century) illustrates the former, and the abbey church of Silvacane (Bouches-du-Rhône) (sec-

---

[43] Reber, p. 342, Fig. 260a. See also, Abbaye de Fontfroide, Baudot and Perrault-Dabot, V, pl. 41.

[44] Found also in St. Paul-Trois-Châteaux, Lasteyrie, p. 412, Fig. 429.

[45] See pp. 13, 14.

[46] Exs., Issoire (Puy-de-Dôme), Saint Paul, see Enlart, I, p. 269, Fig. 102, or Choisy II, p. 209. Toulouse (Haute-Garonne), Saint Sernin, see Choisy, II, p. 212. Culhat (Puy-de-Dôme), Ch. Lasteyrie, p. 250, Fig. 241. Parthenay-le-Vieux (Deux-Sevres), Notre Dame, ill. in Choisy, I, p. 205, etc.

[47] Enlart, I, p. 267, Fig. 100 and Lasteyrie, p. 413, Fig. 430.

The clerestory at Vaison is hardly worthy of the name, for its windows are cut entirely *above* the imposts of the vault, which is of pointed section, and therefore does not acquire thickness so rapidly as to render the windows too deep to admit a reasonable amount of light. The construction of such a clerestory consists merely in taking advantage of the pointed form of vaulting without presenting structural advances. Its windows are necessarily small and deep set and the system is not a satisfactory solution of the lighting problem.

ond half of the twelfth century)[48] the latter form. The advantage of the three-quarter type lies in the fact that it exerts less thrust against the inner wall than does the half tunnel and still makes possible loftier arches in the nave arcade compared to the height of the aisle vault than does the full tunnel vault. But these slight advantages are offset by its ugly appearance, and it was never in any sense popular.

PROVENCE CHURCHES OF THE FIFTH TYPE

The system of the fifth type of the school of Provence is that of a tunnel vaulted nave with side aisles covered by transverse tunnel vaults. This method is, however, so different from the other four and was so widely extended,—largely through Cistercian influence—that it can hardly be said to be inherent in any one school, but rather to constitute an individual group of churches which will be separately considered.

From the foregoing discussion of the entire school, it will be seen that the builders of Provence produced very little that was original in vault construction. It was not a school of progress, but rather one of conservative adherence to the Roman tradition of the province around which it centered. Its most progressive feature was, perhaps, the preference it displayed for the pointed tunnel vault,[49] and this may be explained by the fact that the vault in Provence generally carries directly the tiles of the roof and less masonry was necessary to carry a pointed vault up into a gable than would have been the case with one of semicircular section. One further preference, which shows the structural sense of the Provence builders, is that for transverse arches under the vaults, which not only make possible lighter masonry in the vaults themselves, but also lessen the centering necessary for their construction.

VAULTS SIMILAR TO THOSE OF PROVENCE IN OTHER ROMANESQUE CHURCHES

Such methods of vaulting as those just described are not confined to Provence. In Poitou, for example, there is a group of churches with half-tunnel vaults in their side aisles. Some of these, like Saint Eutrope at Saintes (Charente-Inférieure)[50] (eleventh century) and Aigues-Vives

---

[48] Revoil, II, pl. XVIII.

[49] Semicircular vaults were sometimes used, however. Example, Saint Paul-Trois Châteaux (Drome), Cath. (first half of the twelfth century), Lasteyrie, p. 412, Fig. 429, etc.

[50] Choisy, II, p. 206, Fig. 14.

(Loir-et-Cher),[51] have corresponding half arches, others, like Parthenay-le-Vieux (Deux-Sèvres),[52] (cir. 1129) have full transverse arches beneath these vaults. Moreover, in Auvergne the triforium is regularly covered with a half tunnel vault buttressing the tunnel vault of the nave, and in a few instances, as at Culhat (Puy-de-Dôme),[53] the side aisles are in one story with similar vaulting. There are also many instances outside of Provence in which the aisles have full tunnel vaults. Between Auvergne and Bourgogne there is an example in the abbey church at Souvigny (Allier) (eleventh century) (Fig. 11), and such a system may quite possibly have been employed in the aisles of Cluny[54] and in those of the choir of Saint Benoît-sur-Loire (Loiret)[55] (second half of the eleventh century). Even in England it occurs in the Tower Chapel at London[56] (begun 1078), and is also found in Poitou at Melle (Deux-Sèvres), Saint Pierre[57] (early twelfth century), where the vaults are pointed, and at Lesterps (Charente),[58] where they are of semicircular section. The three-quarter tunnel vault also is not confined to Provence for it appears as far north as Saint Genou (Indre) in the eleventh century.

The foregoing examples serve only to indicate that such systems as these which are inherently simple in construction came, very naturally, to be widely employed during the Romanesque era. Where they originated it is impossible to say, but the fact that they are so elementary in principle and often vary in some of their structural characteristics[59] may indicate that they were developed independently and contemporaneously in various localities.

NAVES WITH TUNNEL VAULTS AND AISLES GROINED

The next three schools of Romanesque architecture have one feature in common, namely, the employment of groined vaults over the side aisles.

---

[51] Enlart, I, p. 268, Fig. 101.

[52] Choisy, II, p. 205, Fig. 13.

[53] Lasteyrie, p. 250, Fig. 241.

[54] See statement to that effect in Rivoira, II, p. 106.

[55] See Dehio and von Bezold, p. 260.

[56] Ruprich-Robert, p. 8, Fig. 45, and Reber, Fig. 235.

[57] Lasteyrie, p. 455, Fig. 473.

[58] Lasteyrie, p. 456, Fig. 474, also Saint Jouin-de-Marnes (Deux-Sèvres), Baudot and Perrault-Dabot, II, pl. 32, and Nouaille (Vienne), Ch., Baudot and Perrault-Dabot, II, pl. 37.

[59] For example, the aisle vaults seldom carry the tile of the roofs outside of Provence and Auvergne.

But the form which these assume and their relations to the tunnel vaults of the nave differ sufficiently to distinguish the churches of Poitou, Auvergne and Bourgogne from one another.

THE SCHOOL OF POITOU

The chronology of the churches of Poitou is somewhat obscure, but the vaulting principles of the school were well developed early in the eleventh

FIG. 11.—SOUVIGNY, ABBEY CHURCH.

century, to which period a number of the existing churches belong. Their naves are tunnel vaulted and without a clerestory, the light entering through windows in the outer walls of the aisles, which are narrow and high and covered with groined vaults rising from the imposts of the arches opening into the nave. The entire church has a single-gabled exterior roof of wood and tile, its rafters supported near their centers by a wall above the nave arcade, and thus not resting directly upon the extrades of the vaults.[60] Certain minor structural differences make it possible to divide the churches of Poitou into two groups.

The first is composed of the earlier churches, of which Saint Savin-sur-Gartempe (Vienne) (begun cir. 1023) is the best and perhaps the only existing example. In it, both nave and aisle vaults are without transverse arches. All the vaults are semicircular in section, and those of the aisles[61] have their transverse surfaces continuous with the soffits of the nave arches.[62] This gives them the flattened groins so characteristic of Roman architecture. Such a system as this required an extensive wooden centering, and it is not surprising that the builders of Poitou soon introduced transverse arches beneath the vaults,—perhaps through the influence of Lombardy, where they were in use as early as the tenth century[63]—thus producing a group of churches which form the second type of the school.

Notre Dame-la-Grande at Poitiers (Vienne) (early twelfth century), is an early example of this class. Transverse arches are employed throughout the church, not only strengthening the vaults but making it possible to save centering by using the same form for each successive bay and at the same time reducing to some extent the thickness of the web by thus breaking it up into smaller units.[64]

Toward the second half of the twelfth century the system was still further improved by the introduction of pointed arches and vaults in both nave and aisles, as for example in the abbey church of Cunault (Maine-et-

---

[60] This arrangement is general in the school and may be understood by referring to the illustration of Melle, Saint Pierre, Lasteyrie, p. 455, Fig. 473. A number of churches which are exceptions to this rule have already been noted under Provence (see pp. 21, 22).

[61] See Lasteyrie, p. 454, Fig. 471.

[62] The three western bays of the church are early twelfth century and have transverse arches.

[63] Rivoira (Rivoira, I, p. 97) says that such arches were used beneath groined vaults as early as the eighth century in the palace of Theodoric at Ravenna, and gives as tenth century examples (p. 176) the aisles of Sant' Eustorgio at Milan and the nave and aisles of S.S. Felice e Fortunato, at Vicenza, and as examples of the early eleventh century, the nave and aisles of San Babila, also at Milan.

[64] It is a question whether the transverse arches actually carried much or any of the weight of the vault. (See discussion of this point as regards crypts in Porter, Construction of Lombard and Gothic Vaults, pp. 17-18.) They did, however, strengthen the church by tying together the piers and walls besides saving centering as above stated.

Loire). The flattened type of groin has here been abandoned, though the vaults are not of domed-up type. Such doming is to be found in Poitou, however, in Saint Pierre at Chauvigny (Vienne),[65] probably with the intention of saving centering, as in Byzantine architecture. But even though the builders of Poitou made some progress in vaulting, they never attempted to solve the associated problem of getting direct light in the nave. Hence such progress was but slight from the earliest to the latest churches of the school.[66]

The School of Auvergne

The Origin and Use of the Triforium Gallery in Auvergne

One of the distinguishing features of the typical churches of Auvergne is the presence of a second story or triforium gallery above the side aisles. To account for its presence a number of theories have been advanced. That such galleries were not intended for congregational purposes, at least in the early churches of the school, is evident from the fact that they are but dimly lighted and accessible only by narrow staircases in dark corners. They may have been used for storerooms or treasuries for relics brought by pilgrims,—a possibility which is strengthened by the fact that they ceased to be built in the thirteenth century when the era of the Crusades was past,[67]—or they may have been useful places from which to defend the church, corresponding in this respect to the room frequently found in the second story of Romanesque towers.[68] But whatever their use, they would seem, in Auvergne, at least, to have originated on purely structural grounds.

The expedient of dividing the openings from the nave of the church to the aisles into two stages, with the evident intention of thus reducing the height of the piers and even of making lighter piers possible, was employed in a number of churches both earlier and later than those in Auvergne. It may even be in part the explanation of the double colonnade in the Lateran Baptistery, and the upper stories in the chapel at

[65] Lasteyrie, p. 455, Fig. 472.

[66] The influence of the Poitou system was quite extensive, however, as is shown by the little church of Saint Loup-de-Naud (Seine-et-Marne) (eleventh and twelfth centuries), Choisy, II, p. 207, Fig. 15.

[67] See Choisy, II, p. 210. The great objection to this is that they are not found in the neighboring provinces, in which much the same reason for having them must have existed.

[68] See Lasteyrie, pp. 388-391, for account of the latter.

Aachen, and the abbey churches at Essen, Nymwegen, and elsewhere. In any case, it explains the system of two stories of arches in the Carolingian church of Saint Michael at Fulda (818-822),[69] and in the early Romanesque churches of Vignory (Haute-Marne)[70] (eleventh century), Montiérender, Haute-Marne)[71] (early eleventh century), and Chatel-Montagne (Allier)[72] (early twelfth century), and probably also in Saint Pierre at Jumièges (Seine-Inférieure)[73] (cir. 940).[74]

A significant fact in connecting these churches which are wooden roofed, with the vaulted churches of Auvergne, lies in their geographical distribution. While the earliest examples such as Fulda lie in the Carolingian region, the latter examples, Jumièges, Vignory and Montiérender lie but slightly north of Auvergne, while Chatel-Montagne is actually in this province.[75] What is more natural to suppose, then, than that the vaulted churches of Auvergne were based upon these earlier churches, and that the nave arcade in two stages was retained even when both aisles and nave were covered with vaults? Furthermore, it would then be perfectly natural that the builders should have built these vaults in two stories corresponding to the two stages of arches, since they would have promptly recognized the great advantage gained by this system, which stiffened the interior and exterior walls for the added weight which the high vaults brought to bear upon them, without injuring to any extent the appearance of the church.[76] This seems all the more plausible when the fact is considered that the churches of Auvergne generally have broader aisles than those of Poitou or Provence. This may also have been a heritage from the early churches with two-storied arcades and wooden roofs just mentioned,[77] and in any

[69] Rivoira, II, p. 283, Fig. 727.

[70] Michel I, p. 444, Fig. 208.

[71] Enlart I, p. 255, Fig. 94.

[72] Lasteyrie, p. 330, Fig. 354.

[73] Rivoira, II, p. 47, Fig. 410.

[74] Other examples showing extent of the method are, Barletta cathedral in Italy, and Rochester Cathedral (twelfth century) in England, while Rouen and Meaux cathedrals furnish Gothic instances. See also Enlart, I, p. 257, note 1.

[75] It is also worthy of note as showing the architectural influence of Lombardy and the Rhenish provinces upon Auvergne, that Chatel-Montagne has the alternate system of supports, a Lombard-Rhenish-Norman characteristic rarely found outside of these schools.

[76] This would also explain the elevation and vaulting of the aisles of Jumièges-Abbey church, which are unlike those of the other churches of Normandy and yet not truly Lombard in type. See p. 43.

[77] It is also characteristic of the churches of Normandy, Bourgogne and the Rhenish provinces, all more or less strongly Lombard.

case it further explains the system of aisle vaults in two stories. For, while the vaults of narrow aisles might be raised a considerable distance from the ground without danger from excessive thrusts, in wide aisles they would have exerted such thrusts and pressures on piers and walls as to have rendered their support most difficult, particularly when they carried directly the tiles of the roof as in Auvergne.

The School of Auvergne continued

As to the actual vaulting system of the Auvergnate churches, it is as follows. In the nave, heavy tunnel vaults resembling those of Provence in that they usually carried the roof.[78] Otherwise the churches are more like those of Poitou in the form of the piers, the almost universal absence of a clerestory, and the employment of vaults of semicircular section with transverse arches, as in the early churches of the second class in that school. In the triforium, the builders realized the advantage gained by the use of a half tunnel vault as an offset to the nave thrusts and as a means of best filling the space beneath a single gable roof,[79] and this is therefore the universal method. At times this vault is borne on full semicircular transverse arches,[80] and at others on those which follow its curve.[81] In the side aisles, groined vaults were employed because they were the only kind which could be built without cutting into either the triforium or the side wall windows. In form they closely resemble those of Poitou and were provided with transverse arches.

Churches of the Auvergne School

The church of Notre Dame-du-Port at Clermont-Ferrand (Puy-de-Dôme)[82] (Fig. 12) (cir. 1100) has the Auvergnate characteristics just described. Its great fault lies in the darkness of the interior, a darkness more pronounced than that of the churches of Provence or Poitou because of the width and lowness of the aisles with the consequent distance of the lateral windows from the nave and the fact that they cannot be cut very

---

[78] An exception to this is to be seen in the church of Champagne (Ardéche), see note 29.
[79] See section of Saint Saturnin (Puy-de-Dôme), Lasteyrie, p. 437, Fig. 454.
[80] Clermont-Ferrand (Puy-de-Dôme), Notre Dame-du-Port, Choisy, II, p. 230, Fig. 30.
[81] Example, Limoges (Haute-Vienne), Saint Martial, Lasteyrie, p. 251, Fig. 242.
[82] See also Issoire (Puy-de-Dôme), Saint Austremoine (early twelfth century), Michel, I, p. 461, Fig. 218. Saint Nectaire (Puy-de-Dôme) (eleventh century).

high above the floor.   The windows of the triforium are also small,[83] and their light is almost entirely confined to the gallery by its floor and by the smallness of the arches opening into the nave.   This fault was rem-

FIG. 12.—CLERMONT-FERRAND, NOTRE DAME-DU-PORT.

edied in the choir, where the light was most needed, by doing away with the triforium, and placing a clerestory beneath the half dome of the apse.[84] As a further improvement a lantern was placed over the crossing.[85]

In certain churches of the school like Saint Sernin at Toulouse (nave twelfth century), the triforium was increased in size, perhaps in order that it might be used for congregational purposes, but more probably be-cause larger windows were absolutely necessary in this portion of the

[83] Partly because the half tunnel vault in this part of the church required a strong and continuous impost.
[84] Already seen in Poitou.
[85] See discussion of this form of crossing on p. 106.

church for the sake of the lighting. This theory is strengthened by the fact that Saint Sernin has double side aisles and the lateral windows are therefore too far away to light the nave. These added aisles are covered with vaults of regular Auvergnate character, even to the extent of half tunnel vaults beneath their roofs, and the remainder of the church corresponds to the structural standards of the school.[86]

CHURCHES OF AUVERGNE WITH A CLERESTORY

Although it might seem from the foregoing pages that the builders of Auvergne were very backward in structural technique, there are a number of churches in the school which have a clerestory in the nave. Among them is Saint Étienne at Nevers (Nièvre)[87] (end of the eleventh century),[88] in which the clerestory is obtained by raising the wall above the triforium arches just high enough to permit the introduction of comparatively small windows with their heads rising above the impost of the vaults.[89] The principle is the same as that in Provence, and no structural innovation is involved. The builders merely relied upon heavy piers and walls and salient buttresses to bear the added thrust which the tunnel vaults, thus raised, produced. That their reliance was not especially well founded is proved by the numerous cracks in the masonry.

THE SCHOOL OF THE LOIRE

The introduction of a clerestory in tunnel-vaulted churches was not yet scientifically accomplished, and it remained for the school of Bourgogne to find the best possible solution of the problem. But this solution would seem to have been reached only after some intermediate steps had been taken which may, perhaps, be traced in a number of eleventh century churches. Two of these lie slightly to the north of Poitou and Auvergne and strongly reflect the influence of these neighboring schools. These churches, together with others in the same general region, may perhaps

---

[86] Saint Sernin served as a model for the Spanish church of Santiago-de-Compostella (eleventh and twelfth centuries), which shows the extended influence of Auvergne.

[87] Other examples are: Chatel-Montagne (Allier), Ch, Chateauneuf (Saône-et-Loire), Ch. Choisy, II, p. 245, Limoges (Haute-Vienne), Saint Martial, (destroyed, see Enlart, I, p. 256, note 5), without windows according to Lasteyrie (see Lasteyrie, p. 251, Fig. 242), Tours (Indre-et-Loire), Saint Martin (probable system).

[88] Illustrated in Baum, p. 154.

[89] See also Chatel-Montagne (Allier), Ch., Lasteyrie, p. 330, Fig. 354.

be said to constitute a school of Romanesque architecture, which might properly be termed the School of the Loire.

The first of these is the small church of Saint Genou (Indre).[90] It is a combination of the types of Auvergne and Poitou except that the tunnel vault of its choir is raised on a clerestory wall pierced with good sized windows. Its aisles are in only one story, and, instead of being groined, are covered by three-quarter tunnel vaults perhaps showing the influence of such Provence churches as those of Silvacane and Vaison. The whole system shows an advance in structural skill in several particulars. In the first place the aisles are built low, and with columnar piers close together, thus insuring the support of a heavy triforium wall. This wall is lightened in appearance but not structurally weakened, by a wall arcade opposite the vaults and roofs of the aisles, and is sufficiently thick at the clerestory level to be pierced with window openings and still afford an excellent impost for the tunnel vault. This, in turn, is built of light material like the vaults of Poitou. With exterior salient buttresses, the system is complete. Its only important drawbacks are the closeness of the supporting piers and the necessity of keeping the whole choir rather low to avoid excessive thrusts.

The second church lies between Saint Genou and the school of Bourgogne. It is the abbey church of Saint Benoît-sur-Loire (Loiret), begun in 1062 and possessing a choir, transepts, and porch, dating from the second half of the eleventh century. Its choir (Fig. 13) closely resembles that of Saint Genou in every particular, except that the aisles have full tunnel vaults and the church as a whole is larger with a much more lofty nave of greater span.[91] Such a system as that of Saint Genou and Saint Benoît is produced by the extension of the elevation so frequently seen in the apses of the churches of Poitou and Auvergne to embrace the sides of the choir as well. The columnar piers and small arches used are like those in the apse rather than like those in the remainder of the church. The builders seem, however, to have failed to realize that walls which would support the half dome of the apse would not necessarily prove sufficiently strong to resist the thrusts of a tunnel vault. In fact, in spite of its apparent advance, the vault of the choir of Saint Benoît was only prevented

[90] Lasteyrie, p. 338, Fig. 360.

[91] The church of Fontgombault (Indre) (Baum, p. 265) is a similar church, but of later date (consecrated 1141), which might be classed as belonging to the "Loire school."

from falling by the addition of transverse arches and flying-buttresses at a date subsequent to the completion of the church, and the vault of the nave of Cluny, which was quite possibly similar, actually fell in 1125.[92]

FIG. 13.—SAINT BENOÎT-SUR-LOIRE, ABBEY CHURCH.

It remained for the twelfth century builders of Bourgogne to take the final steps which were to carry the system of tunnel vaulted naves with direct light to its highest development.

THE SCHOOL OF BOURGOGNE

It is most unfortunate for a study of the school of Bourgogne that the mother church at Cluny (Saône-et-Loire) should have been almost totally destroyed in the French Revolution. This great church was begun in 1089 and must have been finished in 1125, for the nave vaults fell in that year and were rebuilt before the final consecration in 11vo. What its original vaulting system was is difficult to say. Reber[93] says that it was probably

[92] See Lasteyrie, p. 424.
[93] Reber, p. 351.

vaulted like the churches of Auvergne with inner aisles in two stories, but Rivoira[94] states that both the nave and aisles had tunnel vaults on transverse pointed arches.   The exterior view,[95] and the model which fortunately remains, would correspond with either arrangement.[96]   The important facts to note are that the nave had a clerestory, and that the nave vault was strengthened on the exterior by carrying up the clerestory walls to exert a downward pressure at its haunch, a most important structural advance over the exterior wall of Saint Benoît-sur-Loire.[97]

The developed system of Bourgogne may be seen to advantage in the abbey church of Paray-le-Monial (Saône-et-Loire) (Figs. 14, 15), which dates from the early twelfth century and is thus only slightly later than

FIG. 14.—PARAY-LE-MONIAL, ABBEY CHURCH.

[94] Rivoira, II, p. 106.

[95] Rivoira, II, p. 106, Fig. 490.

[96] The plan as given in Guadet, p. 265, Fig. 1127, shows groined vaults in both aisles, and the portion of the church remaining would make it seem probable that it originally had groined aisles in one story, but the matter is of little importance here.

[97] Lasteyrie is of the opinion that these walls were raised to make it possible to place straight wooden beams across the church above the vaults (see Lasteyrie, p. 340, and also Choisy, II, p. 162, Fig. C.), but even if this were one reason, they also materially aided by their downward pressure, in offsetting the outward thrust.

Cluny itself. Its nave is wider and loftier than any yet seen in which a tunnel vault was used, though not equal in size to that at Cluny, which was thirty-two feet wide and ninety-eight feet high. All the structural arches are pointed, but those used for windows, doors and decoration are still round headed.[98] The clerestory, while it has only moderately large windows, is so high above the ground as to render the support of the vaults above it exceptionally difficult. This difficulty was overcome, first by giving the vault a pointed section and thus reducing the thrust; second, by building as light a web as possible and covering it with a wooden roof; third, by using tie-rods of wood or metal, running along near the impost of the vault in the thickness of the walls, thus to a certain extent con-

FIG. 15.—PARAY-LE-MONIAL, ABBEY CHURCH.

centrating the pressure upon the piers; and, finally, as has already been stated, by carrying the exterior walls of the church to a point considerably above the window heads (Fig. 15), thus obtaining a downward pressure which offsets the outward thrusts.

[98] Pointed nave arcade arches were used as early as the eleventh century in Bourgogne in such churches as Farges and Saint Vincent-des-Prés (Saône-et-Loire); see Lasteyrie. p. 428.

The side aisles of the school of Bourgogne are also worthy of mention. They are usually covered with groined vaults, in many cases of slightly domical form. Whether this method came directly from Lombardy where there exist early examples of its use, or whether it came in through the influence of Poitou and Auvergne which had come into close contact with Carolingian architecture, is an open question. It seems quite likely, however, that, since the Byzantine builders developed this type and transmitted it to the Carolingian builders of the Rhine valley, it should have passed from there into France and spread over the three northern-central schools as it did over Lombardy. Regardless of its origin, it became the standard type in all the important churches of the Cluniac region. Occasionally, as at Souvigny (Allier) (possibly eleventh century), the enclosing arches are of stilted round headed form, a type which is also found as far north as Vézelay (Yonne) La Madeleine (after 1140) (Fig. 16). Neither of these churches, however, is near the center of the school,[99] and the pointed structural arch as used in the abbey church of Paray-le-Monial (Fig. 14) is the common form.

The system employed in Bourgogne marks the highest development attained in the use of a tunnel vault running the length of the nave. In the Ile-de-France a few instances might be cited[100] in which a system like one of those already described was used, and the same is true of certain Romanesque churches outside of France, but in none of them is any new structural method introduced. The tunnel vault was even used occasionally as late as the thirteenth century,[101] but the examples are generally small and insignificant.

Churches with Transverse Tunnel Vaults Over the Nave

Besides the methods which have just been described and which were so localized as to form veritable Romanesque schools, there remain a number of churches falling into two groups in which transverse tunnel vaults replace those running longitudinally either in the nave or aisles. The first and smaller group contains those in which such vaults were used over the nave. Of these, the most important example is Saint Philibert at Tournus

---

[99] These lie along the line between Bourgogne and Auvergne, and the influence of the latter school may account for the preference shown in them for round headed arches.

[100] See Enlart, I, p. 275.

[101] Azy (Aisne), Chapel. Jouaignes (Aisne), Chapel. See Enlart, I, p. 445, note 1.

(Saône-et-Loire),[102] a church of considerable size and of early date (dedicated 1019).   Cylindrical piers and transverse arches divide the nave into rectangular bays each of which is covered by a transverse tunnel vault with a window in the clerestory wall at either end.   Excellent light is

FIG. 16.—VÉZELAY, LA MADELEINE.

thus obtained and the thrusts of the vaults admirably counteract one another.   In fact, the system is so logical that it is surprising that it gave rise to so few imitators.[103]   The explanation may perhaps lie in the lack of apparent continuity in the vault, a fault which this method shares with that of Le Puy.   As to its origin, it may go back to such Persian monuments as Tag-Eivan, or to Syrian copies of Sassanian work with the substitution of stone for brick as Choisy suggests,[104] though it is not

[102] Enlart, I, p. 270, Fig. 103, and Porter, I, p. 278.
[103] A few examples are found, among them: Mont Saint Vincent (Saône-et-Loire) Ch. (eleventh century), see Enlart, I, p. 272, and Lasteyrie, p. 248; Palognieu (Loire) Ch. (twelfth century), Enlart, I, p. 272, and Michel, I, p. 475; see also Enlart, I, p. 272, for other examples.
[104] Choisy, II, p. 198.

unreasonable to think that the builders of Tournus originated the system since it involved no unknown structural principles. The aisles of Saint Philibert furnish one of the rather rare examples of the employment of interpenetrating vaults.[105]

CHURCHES WITH TRANSVERSE TUNNEL VAULTS OVER THE AISLES

The second group is much larger and more widespread, and comprises all the churches employing transverse tunnel vaults over the side aisles. The examples belonging to the school of Perigord have already been discussed,[106] and mention has been made of the fact that there are possibly enough of such churches in Provence alone to constitute a fifth type in that school.[107] But the system is too widespread to be attributed to any one province. It is undoubtedly a product of Roman and very early mediaeval architecture, for it is to be seen in such buildings as the Basilica of Maxentius at Rome, and in a modified, ramping form at Aachen.[108] Its structural advantage lies in the large space which the tunnel vault affords for windows in the outer wall thus lighting both the nave and aisles. Among the many examples are the parish church of Chatillon-sur-Seine (Côte-d'Or)[109] of the twelfth century, the abbey churches of Hauterive (Savoie), Ronceray[110] (vaulted in 1115), Bénévent-l'Abbaye (Creuse),[111] and the cathedral of Lescar (Basses-Pyrénées),—in which, however, the vaults are an addition to a primitive construction.[112] In the church at Fontenay (Côte-d'Or)[113] (before the middle of the twelfth century) concealed flying buttresses appear over the transverse arches between the aisle bays, thus aiding in securing a more even abutment for the continuous thrust of the tunnel vault of the nave. A few churches like Cavaillon,[114]

---

[105] See also Saintes (Charente-Inférieure) Saint Eutrope (Crypt of the twelfth century restored in the thirteenth), Enlart, I, p. 294, Fig. 120 bis; Poitiers, Saint Hilaire (aisles added in the nave), Choisy, II, p. 199, Fig. 9.

[106] See p. 5.

[107] See p. 21.

[108] This was also the original method of vaulting in the aisles of the wooden roofed basilica church of Saint Front at Perigueux (cir. 988-991), according to Rivoira, II, p. 113.

[109] Enlart, I, p. 271, Fig. 104, and Michel, I, p. 475, Fig. 236.

[110] Dehio and von Bezold, I, p. 258.

[111] Lasteyrie, p. 249, Fig. 239.

[112] See Lasteyrie, p. 248, and note 3.

[113] Section in Dehio and von Bezold, I, p. 529.

[114] Borrmann and Neuwirth, II, p. 163.

and the cathedral of Orange (Vaucluse),[115] have tunnel vaults over rectangular bays flanking the nave but not connected by arches to form side aisles.

The vaulting of the ambulatory gallery of Mantes cathedral, of the aisles of Fountains Abbey in England, and possibly the original vaults of the aisles of Saint Remi at Reims[116] were also transverse tunnel vaults. These latter churches differ from the ones previously mentioned, however, in that they are not tunnel vaulted in the nave and, moreover, are constructed with a clerestory so that the side aisle vaults do not serve the purpose outlined in the account of tunnel vaulted churches in the preceding paragraph.

Tunnel Vaults with Cross Ribs

This brings the discussion of the standard methods of tunnel vaulting to a close, but there remain two curious churches in which cross-ribs were added beneath the surface of simple tunnel vaults. One of these is at Lusignan (Vienne),[117] and the other at Javarzay (Deux-Sèvres). Both date from about 1120 to 1140 though the ribs may be a later addition to give the appearance of ribbed vaulting which was introduced at about this time.

Naves with Groined Vaults

Although usually confined to the side aisle bays, there are a few Romanesque churches in which the builders of the eleventh and twelfth centuries placed groined vaulting over the nave. The scarcity of such examples is due primarily to the difficulty of meeting the severe outward thrusts of a groined vault raised over bays of considerable span and at a point high above the ground. In the side aisles where the vaults were comparatively low, the exterior wall could be thickened by salient buttresses, and the piers strengthened by the weight of the wall above in a manner to offset the thrust, but in the nave the problem was more complicated. The builders had not yet invented the flying buttress. Hence, when they attempted groined vaults at all, they blundered along trusting that the inert mass of their walls and such timid buttresses as could be

[115] Enlart, I, p. 239.
[116] According to Reber (p. 367), but according to Rivoira (Vol. II, p. 117) they were originally wooden roofed.
[117] Lasteyrie, p. 261, Fig. 251.

erected above the nave piers would provide sufficient offset for the thrusts even though these were now concentrated at four main points in each bay. Naturally the vaults frequently gave way and had to be reconstructed. In spite of these difficulties, the advantage of the groined vault in providing a clerestory whose windows might rise as high as the crown of the vault itself led to its occasional use.

Groined Vaults Over Rectangular Nave Bays

The vaults thus employed were of two rather distinct classes, those over rectangular nave bays which were usually but little domed up, and those over square bays which were generally distinctly domed in the Byzantine manner. Of the first type perhaps the best known example is the Burgundian church of La Madeleine at Vézelay (Yonne), (Fig. 17) dedicated

Fig. 17.—Vézelay, La Madeleine.

in 1104. Its nave is divided into a series of rectangular bays by transverse arches of semicircular section, and over each bay is placed a groined vault very slightly domed at the crown. To insure the stability of these vaults, the builders relied on the weight of the walls, which were carried up some-what above the window heads, and on simple salient buttresses. To these exterior supports were added interior arches half imbedded in the walls above the clerestory windows (Fig. 17), furnishing one of the earliest examples of the use of wall ribs or formerets. The web of the vault does not, however, follow their extrados, but gradually breaks away from it toward the crown, with the apparent object of thus concentrating even more pressure upon the piers by stilting the wall line of the vault surface.[118] Even these precautions were not deemed sufficient, so iron tie-rods were employed, but these rusted and broke,[119] the vaults settled badly,[120] and if it had not been for the addition of exterior flying buttresses, which had meanwhile come into general use, the vaults would most certainly have fallen. Although not a structural success, Vézelay did prove of advantage in turning the builders away from the tunnel vault,—and this, too, in Bourgogne where it had been most highly developed,—to a new type which presented problems whose solution was to lead to Gothic architecture. Vézelay was, however, but little imitated in the Romanesque era, perhaps because of the almost contemporary development of the ribbed vault in Lombardy, Normandy, and the Ile-de-France. A few churches, such as Anzy-le-Duc (Saône-et-Loire)[121] did employ groined vaults over the nave but on a smaller scale and frequently with more pronounced doming.

A more important and independent group of groined vaulted churches is to be found in Normandy. In this school, the churches were usually covered with wooden roofs though the aisles were occasionally groined. But there are three churches in which the choir also has groined vaults. These are, La Trinité or the Abbaye-aux-Dames at Caen (Calvados) (cir. 1066), Saint Nicolas at Caen (cir. 1080), and Saint Georges-de-Boscher-ville at Saint Martin-de-Boscherville (Seine-Inférieure) (late eleventh and early twelfth century). The choir of the third of these churches, though later in date than the others, is more primitive in type, for it is covered by interpenetrating vaults, in which, however, the deep lunettes above the

---

[118] Common to many transitional vaulting systems. See Porter, Cons. of Lombard and Gothic Vaults, pp. 12-14.

[119] Viollet-le-Duc, IV, p. 26.

[120] This can be seen by a glance at the transverse arches as shown in Fig. 17.

[121] See Lasteyrie, p. 427. Other examples are: Pontaubert (Yonne) Ch., Enlart, I, p. 277, Figs. 109-110; Gourdon (Saône-et-Loire) Ch., Lasteyrie, p. 255, Fig. 246; Toulon-sur-Arroux (Saône-et-Loire) Ch. Bragny-en-Charollais (Saône-et-Loire) Ch.

windows rise so nearly to the crown that the result resembles groined rather than tunnel vaulting.

In both the other examples true groined vaulting is used, but at La Trinité it is in practically square bays, and carried by walls running down to the ground,[122] making it easier of construction than that at Saint Nicolas[123] where the bays are rectangular and the choir has true side aisles. This church is similar in structural principles to La Madeleine at Vezelay—except that the wall ribs are omitted,—and these two churches may be said to represent the highest point reached by groined vaulting with practically flat crowns during the Romanesque period.

Other examples might be cited, ranging from such an unusual church as Saint Loup-de-Naud (Seine-et-Marne) in the Ile-de-France,—which is of uncertain date,[124]—to churches as late as the thirteenth and fourteenth centuries, among which are Severac-le-Château (Aveyron) and Saint Pons-de-Mauchiens (Hérault).[125] Occasionally, also, groined vaults were used in the crypt as at Saintes (Charente-Inférieure),[126] even when tunnel vaults were used in the upper part of the church, a peculiarity explained by the fact that underground it was easy to dispose of the thrusts which could not so readily be offset in the nave.

The question of the origin of the method has frequently arisen and a number of writers, including Choisy,[127] suggest the East as a possible cradle of the style because of the numerous churches in Palestine thus vaulted, but Rivoira[128] shows rather conclusively that it was the Cluny influence which carried the method to the East rather than the reverse, a theory strengthened by the fact that the earliest example there, which is the church of Saint Anne at Jerusalem,[129] would seem to be after rather than before the beginning of the twelfth century.[130] Moreover it is quite reasonable to attribute the development of this advanced type of vault to

[122] The side aisles of La Trinité are shut off from the choir and covered with tunnel vaults, a method which is sometimes found in this school. See Ruprich-Robert, I, p. 61.

[123] Bond, p. 293.

[124] See Lasteyrie, p. 540.

[125] See Enlart, I, p. 445, note 2.

[126] Choisy, II, p. 206, Fig. 14.

[127] See Choisy, II, pp. 220-222.

[128] See Rivoira, II, p. 122.

[129] Dehio and von Bezold, I, p. 414.

[130] See Dehio and von Bezold, I, p. 415.

the builders of Bourgogne themselves, for they were surely progressive enough to have taken such a step.

Groined Vaults over Square Nave Bays

Churches with groined vaults over square nave bays are much more numerous than those with rectangular bays, just described. The most important of these belong to the school of the Rhenish Provinces, which had, perhaps, clung to Byzantine and Carolingian traditions in this respect. As a rule the large churches of this school were originally planned for vaulting only in the side aisles.[131] These were usually divided into square bays by round headed transverse arches, and then each bay covered by a more or less domed up groined vault, which, from its size and form, might be erected with comparatively little centering.[132] There was no triforium gallery, but a wall with blank arches took its place beneath the clerestory windows. In many of the churches[133] shafts were carried up on the inner face of alternate nave piers, probably to support the cross beams of the roof, or possibly to carry transverse arches, but not to carry vaulting.

By the early twelfth century, after numerous fires had played havoc with the churches, the Rhenish builders seem to have at last made an effort to replace the wooden roofs with vaults. In doing this, they sought a form of vault which would exert as little as possible of outward thrust and thus be stable at the considerable height at which it must be placed. The Lombard builders had by this time developed the domed up cross-ribbed vault, but, as has been admirably shown by Porter,[134] the ribs which they employed had for their sole purpose the saving of wooden centering, since the masonry of the vault proper was heavy enough to stand without their aid. It was natural then for the Rhenish builders, who copied their neighbors in Lombardy in many particulars,[135] to look to them for a method of vault construction, which they found in domed up vaults like those of Rivolta-d'Adda (1088-1099) or Sant'Ambrogio at Milan

---

[131] The abbey church of Laach (begun in 1093 but work neglected somewhat until its resumption in 1112) is an exception, having been planned from the ground for vaulting. This is not of domed-up type, but seems to have been inspired directly by that of Vezelay. See Rivoira, II, pp. 330-331 and Fig. 781.

[132] See Laach, Abbey Ch. south aisle in Rivoira, II, p. 328, Fig. 777.

[133] Mainz, Speyer, etc.

[134] See Porter, Cons. of Lombard and Gothic Vaults.

[135] Alternate piers, eaves-galleries, etc.

(cir. 1098). These the Rhenish builders chose as models, but being plentifully supplied with wood for centering, it would seem as if they purposely did not adopt the diagonal ribs, but built groined vaults of simple domed up type, placing them over square nave bays each corresponding to two aisle bays in the true Lombard manner. This system may be seen to advantage in the cathedral of Speyer[136] (probably vaulted cir. 1137-1140). With extremely heavy walls like those of the Rhenish churches, and with good masonry for their construction, such vaults proved comparatively safe even over naves of such a span as that of Speyer which is almost fifty feet in width.

This account of the Rhenish school completes the discussion of groined vaulting as applied to the naves and choirs of Romanesque churches. The heavy walls and the general excellence of masonry construction which they required, together with the necessity for large interior piers, did not render them popular or widely used.

AISLES WITH GROINED VAULTS IN LOMBARDY AND NORMANDY

That the use of groined vaults was far more extensive in the aisles than in the naves of Romanesque churches has already been shown by the examples cited from the schools of Poitou, Auvergne, Bourgogne, and elsewhere. To these should be added a number of churches, chiefly of the schools of Lombardy and Normandy, which have groined aisles in combination with rib vaulted or wooden roofed naves. In Lombardy, where the naves are ribbed, this combination has been admirably explained by Porter[137] in connection with the use of wood for centering. Thus he shows that groined vaults, provided that they were sufficiently domed up, could be built over the small bays of the aisles and triforia with almost no wooden framework, but that when such vaults were attempted in the nave the bays were so large as to require a considerable amount of centering beneath the vault, and therefore the builders substituted permanent diagonal arches of very heavy character.

The Norman groined aisles are, however, of a different sort, for they either have level crowns or are but slightly domed up in type.[138]

---

[136] See also Cologne, Saint Maurice (before 1144) Lasteyrie, p. 518; Brauveiller; Guebviller; Rosheim; Schlestadt; Saint Die. See Enlart, I, p. 279, note 2.

[137] Porter, Cons. of Lombard and Gothic Vaults, pp. 20-21.

[138] See aisles of Bernay (Eure), Abbey Ch., Ruprich-Robert, I, p. 61.

The abbey church of Jumièges (Seine-Inférieure) (1040-1067) is among the earliest examples of this construction and is the only Norman church with groined vaults in both the aisles and triforium.[139] La Trinité at Caen[140] and the abbey church of Lessay (Manche)[141] are also Norman churches with groined aisles, in both cases with level crowns. In La Trinité, as in the early churches of Poitou, the bays are not even separated by transverse arches.[142] In Saint Étienne at Caen, and in the choir of the cathedral of Gloucester, the aisles are vaulted in both stories like those of Auvergne, the lower groined, the triforia with half tunnel vaults, but it seems very probable that these latter were added only when vaulting took the place of the wooden roof in the central portions of the church.[143]

Curious instances of the persistence of groined vaulting are to be seen in the triforia of such transitional churches as Saint Germer-de-Fly (Oise)[144] and Vézelay, where the remaining portions of the church have ribbed vaults. For this persistence an explanation is later attempted.[145]

Aisles with Semi-Groined Vaults

An unusual form of aisle vault appears at Creully (Calvados)[146] (twelfth century), where the aisles are covered with a half tunnel vault intersected toward the outer wall by lunettes, which thus convert it into a semi-groined vault. Its obvious advantage lies in the combination of inward pressure, which it exerts in support of the nave vaults, with the added window space which it affords without increasing the height of the exterior walls.

Ribbed Vaults

The introduction of ribs beneath the diagonal intersections of groined vaulting gradually brought about a revolution in Mediaeval building, and transformed the massiveness of Romanesque construction into the light

---

[139] Although this arrangement would seem to reflect Lombard influence, the form of the triforia and of the vaults is much more like those of Auvergne.

[140] Illustrated in Bond, p. 293.

[141] Illustrated in Bond, p. 293.

[142] See also the aisles of Bernay choir in Ruprich-Robert, I, p. 61.

[143] In St. Étienne at least. Gloucester cathedral may or may not have been vaulted before the transformation of its interior from Romanesque to Perpendicular Gothic.

[144] See Fig. 63.

[145] See p. 101, 102.

[146] Ruprich-Robert, pl. LXXXVII.

and graceful architecture of the Gothic era. Much has been written in an effort to discover the origin of the new system. It is not, however, the intention here to add to the number of theories advanced, except in an incidental manner, but rather to classify the various forms of ribbed vaulting as applied to naves, choirs, and aisles of the churches following immediately after those of the Romanesque period which have just been described. As a geographical basis is no longer practical for such a classification, because of the widespread distribution of the new method of construction, a structural basis will be substituted, and the vaults will be divided into two major groups according as they were used over square or rectangular nave bays, and then subdivided according to their minor characteristics.

Ribbed Vaults Over Naves with Square Bays

Lombardy affords the first examples of ribbed vaults over nave bays of square plan. According to Rivoira[147] the earliest are in the church of Santa Maria e San Sigismondo at Rivolta d'Adda[148] (before 1099), though this was closely followed by the more important church of Sant' Ambrogio at Milan (between 1088-1128) (Fig. 18), which furnishes an admirable example of the Lombard type. Its nave is divided into four great square bays, each corresponding to two bays in the side aisles. (Plate I-a.) Of these the eastern bay is treated as a crossing and covered by a dome above a lantern on squinches, but the remaining three have four-part domed up vaults with heavy ribs of square section, used not only transversely and along the walls but also diagonally, thus forming a complete system or skeleton of arches beneath the vault surface in the manner of true Gothic architecture. But there are many reasons to believe with Porter[149] that the builders of Lombardy employed these ribs purely as a permanent centering of masonry,—which was less expensive than a temporary centering of wood in a country where the latter material was very scarce,—and that they failed to appreciate the fact that such ribs made possible a great reduction in the weight of the panels, or web. of the vault, and in other ways could be made to aid in reducing and concentrating its pressures. The masonry of the vault is still excessively

---

[147] Rivoira, I, p. 225.
[148] Rivoira, I, p. 224, Figs. 330, 331.
[149] Porter, Cons. of Lombard and Gothic Vault.

PLATE I

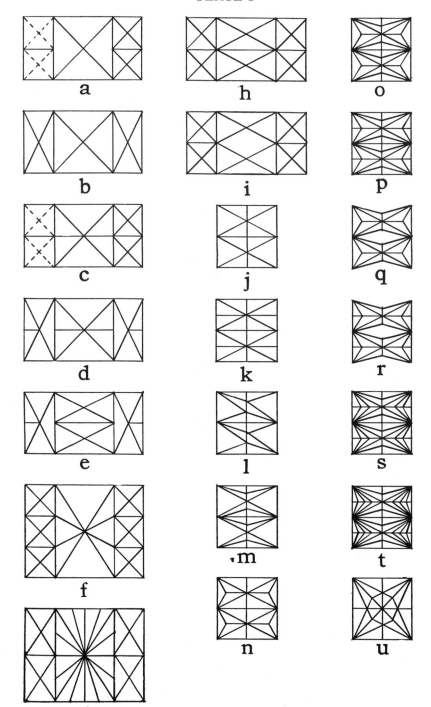

thick,—between sixteen and twenty inches,—and would stand equally well were the ribs removed. Moreover its thrust is so great that the builders dared not raise its imposts sufficiently high to admit of a clerestory beneath the formerets, and instead of rendering possible a lighter construction as Gothic vaults were destined to do, these vaults of Saint'Ambrogio re-

FIG. 18.—MILAN, SANT' AMBROGIO.

quired for their support a wall forty inches thick and ramping walls above the transverse arches of the triforium together with interior tie-rods and wooden chains in the masonry[150] to offset their severe outward thrust. All these facts show that the Lombard vaults are still fundamentally Romanesque in type. Even in San Michele at Pavia (early twelfth century), where the system was a little more developed, in that a small clerestory was introduced, the principles were still the same as in Milan. As a matter of fact, the Lombard builders never made any further advance in the handling of ribbed vaults, and even went backward rather than forward. For the builders found that groined vaults of domed up type could be built so lightly as to require but little centering, and a return

[150] Porter, Cons. of Lombard and Gothic Caults, p. 22.

to this simple form was made in such churches as San Lanfranco at Pavia.[151] Later on, in the thirteenth and fourteenth centuries, French methods of ribbed vaulting were introduced, but throughout the whole period of Lombard supremacy the tendency was to avoid vaulting entirely, and when adopted, it was of the heavy character just described.

The System of Alternate Supports

The Lombard churches are important in the present connection, however, because of the method in which they are divided into vaulting bays. They furnish the earliest examples of the system of alternate light and heavy supports,—employed according to Cattaneo[152] as early as 985 in the three original bays of SS. Felice e Fortunato at Vicenza. This system of piers with alternate transverse arches produces one square[153] bay in the nave to two square bays in the side aisles, and it occurs not only in vaulted churches but also in others in which a wooden roof rests upon these transverse supports.[154] Its advantage in the vaulted churches is particularly important, however, and of a two-fold character. In the first place, it renders the four enclosing arches uniform, and it makes them as nearly as possible of equal span with the diagonals.[155] And in the second, it saves a considerable amount of centering by rendering possible the construction of a vault covering a space corresponding to two rectangular bays on four instead of seven ribs.[156]

Outside of Lombardy, the four-part cross-ribbed vault over square nave bays was but seldom employed in churches with side aisles also divided into square compartments. It appears, however, in the cathedral of Le Mans, (Sarthe) (middle of the twelfth century), where it would seem to be due to the influence of the neighboring single aisled churches of Anjou,—which

[151] Porter, Cons. of Lombard and Gothic Vaults, p. 23.

[152] See Cattaneo, p. 227.

[153] The word square is used to denote bays which are approximately as well as actually equilateral.

[154] See list in Enlart, I, p. 264 note 2 and note 3. Examples of transverse arches of earlier date exist in Syrian and Early Christian architecture, but not with a regular alternate system.

[155] This was especially important to the Lombard builders, who always preferred the semicircular arch, which could thus be employed for all six ribs of the vault and would cause the crown to be domed up just high enough to permit the construction of the entire vault by means of a simple centering from rib to rib. See Porter, Cons. of Lombard and Gothic Vaults.

[156] See Porter, Cons. of Lombard and Gothic Vaults.

are later discussed,—and it was frequently used in reconstructing the vaults of the Rhenish school. In the Gothic period also, the system occasionally appears in a modified form, and naturally enough these revivals occur where Norman and Rhenish Romanesque had caused the principles of Lombard architecture to be strongly entrenched. Thus the church of Saint Legerius at Gebweiler[157] (cir. 1182-1200) furnishes a Rhenish, and the choir of Boxgrove Priory church (cir. 1235), an English application of this method. In the latter, the vaults are no longer highly domed up, and are therefore far removed from their Lombard prototypes, only the general division of the church reflecting this influence.

NAVES WITHOUT SIDE AISLES

More important by far, are the churches without side aisles but with naves in square bays with four part cross-ribbed vaults. This method is to be seen in the cathedral of Fréjus (Var),[158] which is considered by Porter[159] to exhibit the earliest extant ribbed nave vaults in France. These are distinctly of Lombard type, and would seem to show a strong Lombard influence entering France from the south. It may possibly be that this same influence followed the route taken earlier by the dome on pendentives, and thus gave rise to the domed up ribbed vault so common in the churches of Anjou.[160] Of these latter, the cathedral of Saint Maurice at Angers (Maine-et-Loire) (Fig. 19), presents perhaps the best existing example. Its nave vaults which date from as early as 1150[161] are among the largest and finest in France, having a span of some fifty-six feet. As in Lombardy, the crown is highly domed up while to facilitate the construction of the web of the vault with the least possible centering, pointed diagonals and enclosing arches are employed. By this means the entire vault was constructed on the ribs with no centering at all for the lower courses, and a simple *cerce,* a device consisting of two curved boards sliding along

---

[157] Illustrated in M. H.

[158] Illustrated in Porter, Cons. of Lombard and Gothic Vaults, Fig. 19.

[159] See Porter, Cons of Lombard and Gothic Vaults, p. 13.

[160] Examples include: Laval (Mayenne), La Trinité; LeMans (Sarthe), La Couture; Poitiers (Vienne), Cath. (portion); Poitiers, Sainte Radegonde; Brantôme (Dordogne), Ch.; Lucheux (Somme), Ch.; Airaines (Somme), Notre Dame.

[161] They are, perhaps, the earliest of the Anjou group. Enlart (Vol. I, pp. 435, note 1 and 445, note 1) gives an earlier date for Lucheux and Airaines, but the appearance of their vaults does not seem to bear out this assertion.

each other, for those near the crown. At the same time the outward thrusts were greatly reduced by the pointed section of the vault.

Anjou Ridge Ribs

Since the Anjou churches possessed naves of wide span, it is not surprising to find that their builders soon added ridge ribs beneath the vault.

Fig. 19.—Angers, Cathedral.

That these were not mere cover-joints to conceal an irregular intersection of the masonry, as Choisy suggests,[162] would seem to be proved by the fact that the courses meet in a straight line at the ridge in by far the greater number of Anjou churches in which they are employed,—for example in La Couture at Le Mans (Fig. 20), Airaines,[163] and numerous churches with small torus ribs, as well as by the fact that such ridge ribs are sometimes omitted even when the masonry is laid up in courses of equal width and therefore interpenetrating at the ridge, as in Avesnières

[162] See Choisy, II, p. 277 and p. 276, Fig. 8—A. B. C.
[163] Enlart, I, p. 437, Fig. 205.

(Mayenne)[164] near Laval. If not, however, primarily a cover-joint, these ribs did at least, possess both a structural and decorative quality. In the first place they helped to keep the keystone of the diagonals rigidly fixed during the building process, and furthermore, they gave an absolutely

FIG. 20.—LE MANS, NOTRE DAME-DE-LA-COUTURE.

straight line to the vault crown which was always difficult to adjust, particularly in a vault of large size. One of the best and earliest examples of the employment of such ribs appears in the nave of Notre Dame-de-la-Couture at Le Mans (Fig. 20) which dates from about 1200, and a later example is afforded by the church of Saint-Avit-Senieur (Dordogne),[165] where the vaults are of the thirteenth century and replace an original series of domes on pendentives of true Perigord type.

In all of the Anjou vaults thus far discussed, the ribs are of comparatively heavy section and placed entirely beneath the vault surface, but

---

[164] Enlart, I, p. 444, Fig. 210. See also p. 446, note 1.
[165] Lasteyrie, p. 474, Fig. 490.

there was to be a decided change in the thirteenth century. It has already been noted that domed up vaults could be erected almost without centering and exerted little if any pressure upon the ribs beneath them. Realizing this, the builders of Anjou soon began to reduce the size of the ribs until they became little more than torus mouldings running along the groin and ridge of the vault. As an actual fact, however, these torus mouldings were carved upon a sunken rib flush with the surface of the panel, which, if it no longer furnished a support for the vault, at least formed a sort of permanent centering dividing the surface to be vaulted into distinct severies and marking the line of their intersection in an absolutely correct curve. Such vaults are closely allied to those of groined type, the ribs playing practically the same part as those of brick in Roman concrete vaulting. Since, however, in the Anjou system the ribs always were merely a permanent centering which could easily be removed without destroying the vault, a sunken centering was quite as efficient in serving the purpose of vault division while the torus afforded a certain amount of surface decoration.

Of this typical Anjou construction, there are numerous examples. At Poitiers, in the church of Sainte Radegonde the ribs are of reduced size but not quite flush with the vault surface and the same is true at Saint-Hilaire—Saint-Florent near Saumur (Marne-et-Loire),[166] while the choir and transept of Angers cathedral (Fig. 19), and the later bays of the cathedral of Poitiers furnish examples of the standard type. After a short period of experiment, the builders of Anjou became very skillful in the construction of these ribs and vaults and frequently employed them over bays of unusual plan and elevation as, for example, in the chapel north of the choir aisle in Saint Serge at Angers (Fig. 21).

An instance of the influence of Anjou construction upon the neighboring territory, as well as of the relationship between this Gothic style and the Romanesque school of Perigord, may perhaps be seen in the Old Cathedral of Salamanca in Spain.[167] Here the three western bays of the nave are covered with ordinary domes but with diagonal ribs beneath them, while the two remaining bays have regular domed up Anjou vaults. The date of this cathedral, cir. 1120-1178, may, perhaps, explain this peculiar combination as being due to an Anjou-Gothic influence displacing one of

[166] Ill. in Bond, p. 328, Fig. 4.
[167] See Street, p. 80, and Fig. 7, opp. same.

Perigord-Romanesque, in much the same manner as such an influence displaced the Perigord-Romanesque architecture of western France.

Square Nave Bays Outside of Lombardy and Anjou

Besides its use in Lombardy and Anjou, the square nave bay with four part cross-ribbed vaults, was employed to some extent in other parts

FIG. 21.—ANGERS, SAINT SERGE.

of Europe throughout the Gothic period.[168] Some of these are churches without side aisles, but aisles are more commonly found, divided into rectangular bays corresponding in number to those of the nave. Of the single naved churches, San Francesco at Assisi,[169] is a good example. Although dating from 1236-1259, its vault ribs are still heavy and almost square in section, as if derived from Lombard prototypes. But they differ in being of pointed section and in not giving to the vaults a domed up crown. In this they would seem to be examples of French influence upon Lombard tradition.

Square Nave and Rectangular Aisle Bays

An early church with square nave bays and ribbed vaults over rectangular bays in the side aisles (Plate I-b), is to be found at Bury (Oise) (Fig.

---

[168] Examples could be cited in Belgium, Holland, Norway, Spain, etc., in fact, wherever Lombard, Rhenish or Anjou influence was strong.

[169] See also Milan, S. Nazzaro. Cummings, I, p. 116.

22). It probably dates from about 1125, and is an important monument of the Transitional period. Its nave vaults are quite highly domed and in this respect seem somewhat Lombard, but their pointed arches and awk-

FIG. 22.—BURY, CHURCH.

ward construction indicate an effort on the part of the builders toward reducing this doming and a dawning consciousness of the value of the pointed arch in the construction of ribbed vaults. This is further shown in the side aisles. Because of the rectangular shape of the bays, .the problem was presented of getting three sets of ribs of different span to rise to the same or practically the same height. Not being thoroughly familiar with the flexibility of the pointed rib, the builders at Bury were, naturally somewhat clumsy in its use. Thus, the diagonals were made segmental in elevation to lower them to the level of the pier arches, while masonry was piled on the crown of the transverse ribs, or their voussoirs widened, to bring them up to the level of the vault panel.[170]   A few such experimental steps as these at Bury, were all that were necessary to give the builders a mastery of the use of the pointed arch in ribbed vaulting.

Ribs with Caryatid Supports

But there is another feature of the side aisle vaults which is worthy of note before turning to the more developed churches which resemble Bury

Fig. 23.—Bury, Church.

in their arrangement of vaulting bays.   This is the use of small caryatid figures which appear at the springing of the diagonal ribs (Fig. 23).[171] These would seem to serve a purely decorative purpose, perhaps to distract attention from the great size of the ribs behind them, or to give an

[170] Similar building-up of the arches may be seen in the nave at Bury (Fig. 22), and in the narthex of St. Leu d'Esserent (Oise). See Moore, p. 68 and p. 69, Fig. 24.

[171] Very interesting examples occur also at Saint Aignan (Loire-et-Cher), Ch.

apparent lightness to the vault itself by seemingly placing its burden upon such insignificant shoulders, or more probably still, the figures served to break the transition from shaft to rib by concealing the impost of the latter. Whatever their explanation, other examples besides those at Bury are to be seen. Of these, the angels—now badly mutilated—at the base of the ribs in the narthex of Saint Ours at Loches (Indre-et-Loire) (Fig. 24)[172] are especially interesting, and perhaps account for the tiny figures

FIG. 24.—LOCHES, SAINT OURS.

employed at the springing of the ridge ribs in a number of churches in Anjou, such as Angers, Saint Serge (Fig. 21), as well as for the larger figures in the apse of Notre Dame-de-la-Couture at Le Mans (Fig. 20).[173] It may even be through the influence of such figures as these that grotesques were used to support the small shafts in the arcade of the triforium passage in the cathedral of Nevers (Nièvre) (Fig. 25).

[172] Similar angels are found in the porch of Santiago-de-Compostella illustrated in Uhde, Baudenkmaeler in Spainen und Portugal; also in Madrazo-Gurlitt, pl. 166. These latter are Angels of Judgment, forming part of the sculptural scheme of the three portals.
[173] Similar figures also appear at Salamanca, in the old cathedral. See Street, p. 80 and Fig. opp. p. 80. Uhde, op. cit., Fig. 119, p. 50.

SQUARE NAVE AND RECTANGULAR AISLE BAYS CONTINUED

Returning to the churches later in date than Bury but vaulted on the same plan, it will be found that there are but few examples in France, an

FIG. 25.—NEVERS, CATHEDAL.

interesting fact for which an explanation will later be attempted.[174] The lower story of the Sainte Chapelle at Paris (cir. 1250) furnishes one of the rare examples, but here the nave and aisles are of the same height and so do not exactly resemble the system at Bury. Because of their narrowness, the side aisle vaults of the Sainte Chapelle did not furnish proper abutment for those of the nave, and the builders found it necessary to add tie-rods and even transverse half arches forming veritable interior

[174] See p. 57.

flying butresses at about half the height of the transverse ribs. This is, however, a most unusual arrangement.

It was in Italy more than elsewhere that the method of square nave and rectangular aisle bays was adopted. Many of the largest churches of the Gothic period in that country were thus constructed. Among these, Santa Maria Novella at Florence (end of the thirteenth and beginning of the fourteenth centuries) has nave bays which are practically square, while the cathedral of Santa Maria del Fiore (fourteenth century) in the same city is a much larger church more strictly following the type.[175] This vast edifice presented such a vaulting problem that the builders did not hesitate to resort to the use of iron tie-rods to counteract the thrusts,— a subterfuge common enough in Italian architecture, of which the church of the Frari at Venice (after 1250) presents an exaggerated example.

Lighting Problems in Naves with Square Bays

Several factors enter into the lack of popularity of the vaulting system just described especially in the more northern countries, but the fundamental one would seem to be the difficulty of properly lighting churches thus covered. If an examination be made of the churches with a single broad nave and no aisles it will be seen that in Italy, where a comparatively small proportion of window space was necessary, the builders were content with a single window in each nave bay as for example, in San Francesco at Assisi. In France, on the other hand, the light thus admitted would have proved inadequate, and in such churches as the cathedral of Angers (Fig. 19) and Sainte Radegonde at Poitiers two windows were introduced under each wall rib. This is, however, an awkward arrangement because these windows do not properly fill the wall space, and though this is better accomplished by adding a circular window above the upright pair as was done in La Couture at Le Mans (Fig. 20), still the effect even then is not satisfactory and much solid wall which might be utilized for windows is wasted. Moreover, in a church with side aisles, the clerestory arrangement was still more troublesome since important structural difficulties were involved. To raise a great four part vault high above the aisles in order to obtain a large

---

[175] Other examples include: Bologna, San Petronio, ill. in Joseph, p. 172, Fig. 132; Verona, Cath. See Bond, p. 321; Pavia, San Teodoro (1150-1180), see Bond, p. 321; Venice, SS. Giovanni e Paolo, Cummings, II. p. 192.

clerestory was no easy task because of the excessive thrust which such a vault exercised at its four points of support. In Italy, where the amount of light required was not great, a very low clerestory with small, circular windows, one to each bay, was all that was essential, and so in such churches as Santa Maria Novella and the cathedral at Florence the nave vault was placed at a point only slightly above the vaults of the aisles, and its thrusts offset by simple ramping walls beneath the side aisle roofs. Such a church in France would have been inadequately lighted, and even if a greater structural skill permitted the French to erect loftier clerestories than those in Italy, there remained the difficulty of arranging the windows to get the maximum of light and the best appearance. A single opening occupying the entire space beneath the wall rib would have been all head and no jamb. One upright window would have admitted too little light for a large nave, and two windows near together not only left a great deal of wall space unused but were most awkwardly placed in churches where one nave bay corresponded to two bays in the aisles as in Le Mans cathedral,[176] because they were not on an axis with the arches of the nave arcade. On the other hand, if placed on this axis, the resulting windows were necessarily of small size like those in such Rhenish churches as the cathedral of Speyer where a second stage of windows has been added one in the center above each lower pair in a far from satisfactory manner since it brings a window above the intermediate pier.

ORIGIN OF SEXPARTITE VAULTING

In view of these facts it is at least a reasonable assumption that the lighting problem had much to do with the discarding by the French builders of the simple square four-part nave vault. As a matter of fact, however, they did not exactly discard it, but evolved from it a vault in six cells, which, while it still retained the old division of the nave into square bays, each corresponding to two bays in the aisle, at the same time permitted the uniform treatment of these in elevation and made possible larger windows,—one to each aisle bay,—symetrically placed and, in the course of time filling the entire space beneath the wall ribs. This six-part ribbed vaulting would seem to have originated early in the twelfth cen-

[176] See also Rivolta d'Adda—Rivoira, I. p 234, Fig. 331; Pavia, S. Michele, Porter, I, ill. 104, opp. p. 204.

tury, in the French province of Normandy. This province has already been mentioned as the center of a Romanesque school, which extended over the greater part of England after the conquest of 1066, and reached its height during the reign of Duke William, the Conqueror (1035-1087), when a vast number of churches were constructed, many of them of large size. These were in general wooden roofed throughout, though, occasionally, as has been shown,[177] groined vaults were used in the choir or aisles, or both. Toward the beginning of the twelfth century, however, the Norman builders determined to vault the naves of a number of these churches, among them the two abbeys at Caen, and the result of this determination was the evolution of the true and false six-part vault.

Like the Rhine provinces, Normandy had always been strongly influenced by the methods of building developed in Lombardy. Whether this was due to the presence in Normandy of such men as Lanfranc,— who was born in Pavia in 1005 and became successively prior of Bec (1045-1066), abbot of Saint Étienne at Caen (1066), and archbishop of Canterbury (1070-1089), and who may have kept Normandy closely in touch with Lombardy,—or whether there were other more powerful influences, it is impossible to state, but in any event the architectural analogies between the two schools are striking. This is especially true of the type of shafted pier most frequently found in Normandy, and of the alternate system of light and heavy supports, which, while it does not characterize all the churches of the school, is found in many of them. Thus when the Norman builders determined to vault their great churches at Caen, one would naturally expect to find them turning to Lombardy for a method of vault construction, especially since Sant' Ambrogio at Milan had been successfully completed at least a quarter of a century before their determination was made. And in fact this is probably what they did. But there were certain differences in structure between the churches of the two schools which made it impossible for the Norman builders to adopt unchanged, the heavy square, domed-up, cross-ribbed vaults of Lombardy. The first of these differences lay in the fact that the Norman churches were originally built for wooden roofs,—which may even have been in place, in many cases, when the vaults were begun,—while the Lombard churches were planned from the ground for their vaulting. The

[177] See pp. 39 and 42.

second difference was, that the Norman interior system possessed a clerestory window of considerable size centered above each of the arches opening into the side aisles,—that is two in each wall of what would be a square nave bay,—while the Lombard churches either had no clerestory at all, as at Sant' Ambrogio, or one in which the windows were small and there was no attempt to center them as in San Michele at Pavia.

It was natural that the Norman builders should have preferred to preserve their interior and exterior elevations as nearly as possible as they were when only a wooden roof was used, both to avoid the expense which would be involved in reconstruction and to preserve the large clerestory so essential in a northern country. To vault these churches and at the same time save this clerestory would seem to have been the problem, therefore, which the builders set themselves to solve. That they attempted to use the four-part vault in its solution will be seen from an examination of the seven vaulted churches[178] still remaining in which the old system of square nave bays is found, for in four of these a variant of four-part ribbed vaulting was employed while in the other three a new method was developed out of the four-part type.

A study of the two abbeys at Caen will illustrate this. Of the two, Saint Étienne or the Abbaye-aux-Hommes (cir. 1064-1066) would seem to be the earlier as far as its vaulting is concerned and this would seem to date from about 1135. In its nave (Fig. 26) the alternate system of supports is employed, though all the piers are of almost the same section with a single shaft carried up the inner face. The aisles are in two stories and there is a clerestory with a single window in each bay. The nave was originally covered with a wooden roof. With this elevation existing before the church was vaulted it is quite possible to account for the form which this vaulting assumed. The first step must have been to divide the nave into square bays by transverse arches,—assuming that these were not already in place. The springing of these arches must naturally have been governed by that of those which opened into the crossing, and the level of their crowns, by the wooden timbering of the roofs,—which may well have been in place when the vaults were built. The result was that these transverse arches had to rise from a point as low as the clerestory stringcourse and could only be a slightly stilted semicircle in elevation. If the

---

[178] Omitting for the present the cathedral of Durham.

bays thus constituted were to be covered by four-part vaults of Lombard type, the next step would have been to erect diagonals of semicircular section thus doming up the vault at the crown, but at Caen such diagonals

FIG. 26.—CAEN, SAINT ÉTIENNE.

would have rendered necessary an entire change in the timbering of the roof because their intersection would have risen above the level of the trusses. Hence segmental diagonals were substituted. Upon this skeleton of ribs, it would have been quite possible to place a four-part vault, but the wall intersection of its panels would have cut off the heads of the clerestory windows. Several methods could have been used to avoid this. In the first place the severies could have been so shaped as to cut the walls in a curve above the window, but this would have given a flattened form to the panel and rendered it most difficult both to construct and to support when in place. A second expedient would have been to reduce the size of the windows but this, besides cutting off most necessary light would have utterly destroyed the splendid proportions between the horizontal divisions of the Norman interior. A third method would have been to move the windows toward the intermediate pier, but this would have destroyed the axis line of the aisle, triforium, and window arches, and was wisely rejected. Lastly the imposts of the ribs could have been raised, but even this would have introduced enormous structural changes: first, because it would have rendered necessary a change in the timbering, or else raising the entire roof of the church; second, because it would have placed the new impost out of level with the crossing arches; third, because it would have greatly increased the thrust of the vault, already most difficult to meet because of the segmental form of the diagonals and the lack of extensive knowledge of buttressing principles on the part of the Norman builders.

To avoid all these difficulties and still retain the windows, a new method of vaulting was evolved. An intermediate transverse arch was added meeting the diagonals at their intersection, and above the triangular window cells thus formed, separate vault panels were constructed (Fig. 26). The line of the window heads was thus left undisturbed and the six-part vault created (Plate I-c).

FALSE OR PSEUDO-SEXPARTITE VAULTING

Of course, the foregoing suggestion that the six-part vault was evolved from four-part vaulting is largely conjectural, but an examination of other churches in Normandy would seem to show that the Norman builders almost always preferred to use the simple four-part vault in a slightly modified form whenever it was possible to do so and still retain the clerestory windows, rather than to employ the developed six-part type. This modified four-part vault may properly be termed false or pseudo-sex-partite. That it was not a mere prototype of the more developed six-part form would seem to be shown by the fact that it was built in churches both contemporary with, and subsequent to those with true six-part vaults.

A good example of pseudo-sexpartite vaulting, for comparison with that of Saint Étienne (Fig. 26), is afforded by La Trinité or the Abbaye-aux-Dames at Caen (Fig. 27). It would seem probable that the upper portions of this church were extensively rebuilt at the time when vaulting was added. In this rebuilding, concealed flying-buttresses were constructed beneath the side-aisle roofs, and these, together with the solid wall which replaces the open triforium gallery of Saint Étienne, made it possible to raise the level of the transverse arches of the vaulting to a point considerably above the clerestory string-course. Furthermore, since the wooden outer roof was probably built after the vaults, it was possible to

FIG. 27.—CAEN, LA TRINITÉ.

use diagonals whose crowns were higher than those of the transverse arches, and still place them beneath the roof trusses. With such a skeleton of ribs as a basis, the builders proceeded to erect a four-part vault over each nave bay, or, in other words, enclosing two side aisle arches. Because of the higher impost of the vault ribs, the wall intersection of the vault cells easily cleared the window heads.[179] Curiously enough, however, the builders connected the intermediate piers with a transverse arch

[179] These windows like others of the Norman school are actually to one side of the center of the bay but not far enough to make the difference apparent. In fact, they would seem to have been moved over for the purpose of making them appear in the center since the inward curve of the diagonal, which lies on one side of them only, would make them appear to be out of center were they placed on the axis of the bay.

having a flat wall built upon it to the level of the crown of the longitudinal vault cells (Fig. 27). There would seem to be several explanations of this innovation. In the first place the pier system of La Trinité is regular, not alternate, and a greater symmetry was obtained by having corresponding transverse arches connecting each pair of opposite piers. Moreover such arches had been used before 1114 in the church of Saint Georges at Boscherville, and quite possibly elsewhere as well,[180] beneath a simple wooden roof, thus tying together the lofty clerestory walls. In the second place, such arches had already been introduced at Saint Étienne, though for a different reason, as has been shown, and must have proved of value in keeping the keystone of the diagonals rigidly fixed, besides having become a characteristic of what was perhaps the major church of the school; and in the third place, such an arch with its wall above aided materially both in carrying a portion of the weight of the vault to the alternate piers and in affording permanent centering, which was needed in Normandy even more than in Lombardy because the Norman vault crown was never more than slightly domed up.

Once introduced, this pseudo-sexpartite vault was not restricted to La Trinité but was, as has been said, employed in no less than four of the seven square-bayed Norman churches. At Ouistreham (Calvados)[181] (vaulted cir. 1160), the impost was raised as in La Trinité and pointed transverse arches were used, thus increasing the curve of the diagonals and improving the stability of the vault. More interesting still, however, are the two churches of Bernières-sur-Mer,[182] and Saint Gabriel (Calvados)[183] (both vaulted cir. 1150), for in them the builders have clung so tenaciously to the pseudo form in preference to the true that they have actually moved the windows of each bay toward the intermediate pier in order to use this method without raising the imposts. The latter is particularly interesting because of the extreme flatness of its diagonals for which the intermediate transverse arches must certainly have proved an added support.

---

[180] Enlart gives several examples, though not in churches with a regular pier system. Among these are: Cerisy-la-Forêt (Manche), Enlart, I, p. 261, Fig. 97; Le Mans, N. D. du Pré (original state); Villemagne (Hérault), Saint Gregoire (ruined), see Enlart, I, p. 264, note 2.

[181] Illustrated in Ruprich-Robert, pl. LXXIX.

[182] Ruprich-Robert, pl. LXXVIII.

[183] Ruprich-Robert, LXXXI.

The preference of the Norman builders for this pseudo-sexpartite vault, even to the extent of moving the windows out of center to make its use possible, may find a further explanation than any yet given in the simplicity of its construction. A comparison of one window severy of Saint Étienne (Fig. 26) with one at La Trinité (Fig. 27) will illustrate this point. In the former the surface of the vault is warped on either side of the window, while in the latter, the stone courses run almost directly back to the wall, so that the line of intersection is approximately the projection of one-half of the diagonal rib. Of course this second surface was far easier to calculate geometrically and could be put in place by less skillful builders than the warped surface required. It had, however, the fault of being in ill accord with the curve of the window head, but, on the other hand, it possessed the structural advantage of distributing the thrust of the vault over a large amount of exterior wall. This might seem a fault rather than an advantage, were it not that in such a primitive system as that of Normandy, thickness of wall was the greatest factor in abutment and thrusts which were widely distributed were thus more easily met than those which were concentrated within narrow perpendicular limits.[184] The advantage of the warped system in thus concentrating the thrusts was, in fact, realized only when inert stability which forms the keynote of Norman work gave way to the carefully balanced thrusts and counter-thrusts of Gothic architecture.

The little church of Le Petit Quévilly (Seine-Inférieure)[185] (cir. 1156) would seem at first to disprove this Norman preference for pseudo-sexpartite vaults. The imposts of its arches are sufficiently high to permit of such a type, yet the real six-part vault was employed. The explanation of this would seem to lie in the geographical situation of the church, for it is not in Calvados, like the other examples, but in Seine Inférieure near Rouen, or in other words on the border of the Ile-de-France, where the six-part vault had been adopted with enthusiasm and used as early as 1140,

---

[184] In England, where thick walls are an important factor in vault support even at a comparatively late date, this same form of vaulting conoid is frequently found, for example in Chichester, Cath. (ill. in Moore, Mediaeval Church Architecture of England, p. 110, Fig. 91), Worcester, Cath. choir, (ill. in Moore, Mediaeval Church Architecture of England, pl. XX), Lincoln, Cath., E. Transept (see Moore, Mediaeval Church Architecture of England, p. 116), etc.

[185] Ruprich-Robert, pl. LXXXVIII.

or some fifteen years previous to the building of Petit-Quévilly, in the large abbey church of Saint Denis.

It is also difficult to explain the use of the true form in the seventh of the vaulted churches, which is that of Creully (Calvados),[186] but the fact that it has the same low imposts as Saint Étienne at Caen combined with the evident purpose of the builders to keep the windows in the center of the bays may perhaps furnish an explanation of its appearance here.

DEVELOPMENT OF SEXPARTITE VAULTING

The true six-part vault, as used in Saint Étienne, was far from being perfect. In the first place, it possessed a number of inherent structural faults. These lie chiefly in the unequal distribution of thrusts, and the unequal size of the panels into which the vault is divided. From an aesthetic point of view, two other faults might be added: first, the decrease in the apparent length of the nave, due to the fact that it was divided into a few large bays, instead of twice as many smaller ones; and second, the fact that the crowns of the vault cells above the windows do not run out perpendicularly from the clerestory wall but at an awkward angle, thus greatly injuring the symmetry of the bays. Yet in spite of these drawbacks, which were common to all six-part vaulting, this system had a long period of popularity. There are, however, certain structural weaknesses in these early Norman vaults which were largely due to lack of experience on the part of the builders, and not to the form of the vaults themselves. Wall ribs were, for example, omitted, and the diagonals were made of segmental section, thus rendering unnecessarily severe the thrusts of the vaults. Moreover, such a church as St. Étienne was not planned from the ground for vaulting and the piers had not the proper arrangement of shafts. Last of all, the intermediate arches were of a rather ugly, stilted character, possibly so constructed with an eye to a better distribution of light, but in any event presenting an awkward appearance. All these faults were gradually overcome in the Transitional and Early Gothic churches of the Ile-de-France.

SEXPARTITE VAULTING IN THE ILE-DE-FRANCE

That it should have been this province which favored the six-part system is most curious, for at a date almost contemporary with St. Étienne at

---

[186] Ruprich-Robert, pl. LXXXVII.

Caen, ribbed vaults of rectangular plan had probably been constructed over the naves of Saint Étienne at Beauvais and the abbey church at Saint Germer-de-Fly (Oise) (cir. 1130-40). That this method was abandoned in most of the remaining Transitional churches would seem to have been due to the fact that the vaults of Saint Étienne at Beauvais fell in, and those of Saint Germer did not prove very secure.[187] Such builders as the Abbot Suger of Saint Denis, therefore, may very naturally have looked to Normandy for a method of vaulting, since the vaults of Saint Étienne at Caen had at least remained in place.

Whatever the cause of its introduction into the Ile-de-France may have been, the six-part system was used at Saint Denis (Seine) (1140-1144) and soon became the favorite method throughout the neighboring region. Unfortunately Saint Denis and two other important churches of the Transition, the cathedrals of Senlis (Oise) (cir. 1150) and Noyon (Oise) (cir. 1140), which would undoubtedly have illustrated the progress in six-part vaulting, no longer have their original vaults, and the cathedral of Sens (Yonne) (1140-1168) (Fig. 28) remains as perhaps the most important example of the early developed type.[188] Its vaults show the great advance made in construction since the completion of Saint Étienne at Caen. The diagonals are semicircular instead of segmental arches, and the transverse ribs are pointed and all of similar curve, giving a more symmetrical appearance and greatly reducing the thrusts. Furthermore the piers are profiled from the ground according to the load which they are to carry, and, last of all, a highly stilted wall rib is added over each clerestory window, completing the skeleton of the vault and making possible a larger expanse of glass and more satisfactory illumination for the interior. Of course, the use of the flying buttress, which had been introduced a short time before Sens was built, contributed enormously to the advancement of vault construction and in large measure explains such an improved form of vaulting as this is. In fact, a heavy clerestory wall was no longer essential to the support of the vault and it was only the fact that a large expanse of glass was not safe from the pressure of the wind, which prevented the clerestory windows from occupying the entire

---

[187] Flying-buttresses had to be added not long after their construction, to keep them from falling.

[188] Even these vaults have suffered from reconstruction in the thirteenth century.

space beneath the formeret. With the invention of tracery, what little wall remained, was to disappear. A further advance is shown in the decidedly stilted form of the wall ribs, which (Fig. 28) concentrate all the thrust of the vault upon a very narrow strip of exterior wall where it was admirably met by the flying-buttress.[189]   In fact, the system at Sens might

FIG. 28.—SENS, CATHEDRAL.

be considered perfected were it not for the unnecessary size of the ribs, especially those running transversely. It remained for the builders of the cathedral of Notre Dame at Paris (begun 1163) to reduce all the ribs to the same size, and for the builders of the cathedral of Bourges (Cher) (begun 1172), still further to reduce all but the transverse arches and to employ the vault upon a scale even greater than that of Paris. In fact, Bourges marks the high water mark of this system of vaulting and by the beginning of the thirteenth century it was in general, entirely given

---

[189] See Moore, p. 130 et seq. for discussion of this point.

up[190] in favor of the four-part cross-ribbed vault of rectangular plan, which regained its supremacy in the Ile-de-France after the introduction of the flying-buttress with the protection which this afforded against such a catastrophe as that which probably befell Saint Étienne at Beauvais.

Although employed to a much greater extent in France[191] than elsewhere, almost every country in Europe possesses a number of churches with six-part vaults. Thus William of Sens introduced the system into England, where it appears in Canterbury cathedral choir (1175) and later in Lincoln transept[192] (cir. 1215). Italy possesses many examples, among them the large churches of San Francesco at Bologna (cir. 1240), the Certosa of Pavia (1396), and the small church of Corneto-Tarquinia (Roma)[193] where the vault curiously enough appears over two bays of rectangular plan which divide what would otherwise be practically a single square nave bay.[194] Examples in other countries might be cited, but in no case would they differ materially from the French prototypes.

VARIANTS OF SEXPARTITE VAULTING

The fact that six-part vaulting declined rapidly in favor toward the beginning of the thirteenth century, and thus before the era of complicated vaults had begun, probably explains the few variants from the standard type. Of these, the simplest consists in the addition of a ridge rib along the longitudinal vault crown. This appears in one bay of the choir of Lincoln cathedral[195] (Fig. 35), where the crown line is horizontal, and in the great transept of the same church where it rises and falls in accordance with the doming up of the central keystone. The small church of Saint Jacques at Reims (Marne) (1183) (Fig. 29) presents a still better example of this irregular ridge rib. The vault of Saint Jacques would seem from its general appearance to be based upon Anjou models and it is not

---

[190] A later instance does appear and this, too, on a very large scale in the rebuilt choir vaults of Beauvais cathedral (1284), but the six-part vaults of this church are entirely due to the subdivision of four-part rectangular vaults in order to obtain greater stability.

[191] Among the more important examples not mentioned are: Laon (Aisne), Cath; Mantes (Seine-et-Oise), Cath.; Dijon (Côte-d'Or), Notre Dame, etc.

[192] Other examples are: Lincoln, Cath. choir: (Fig. 35) Durham, Cath. east transept; Rochester, Cath. presbytery, (Moore, Mediaeval Church Architecture of England, pl. XVIII), etc.

[193] Porter, Cons. of Lombard and Gothic Vaults, Figs. 58-60.

[194] Other Italian examples are: Casamari, Ch.; San Galgano, Ch.; San Martino, Ch.; etc.

[195] This bay was rebuilt (cir. 1237-1239) after the fall of the tower and is, therefore, later than the transept (cir. 1200).

surprising to find its possible prototype in the church of La Trinité at
Angers (Fig. 30). The reason for the employment of the extra rib is
probably twofold: first, to lessen the size of the transverse panels; and
second, to render the arrangement of the ribs and severies more sym-

FIG. 29.—REIMS, SAINT JACQUES.

metrical. In England, it is quite possible that it served as a cover-joint
as well, but in France this would not seem to hold true, at least in La
Trinité, where the stone courses are laid with as much care as those in
the simple four-part vaults of Angers cathedral (see Fig. 19).

La Trinité at Angers (Fig. 30) is also an important variant of the
six-part vault because the impost of its intermediate rib is raised to a
considerably higher level than that of the principal transverse arches and
the intermediate rib itself is highly stilted. This would seem further evi-
dence that the six-part vault was evolved from the four-part vault in an
effort to make the arrangement of the windows more symmetrical in a
single nave bay corresponding to two bays in the aisles;[196] for if La

[196] In La Trinité there are no side aisles, but a series of chapels constitutes virtually
the same arrangement.

Trinité with its series of side chapels, two to each nave bay, had been vaulted in the usual Anjou style and the windows left as they now stand on the axis of each chapel arch, their heads would either have been cut by the wall line of a four-part vault or would have appeared awkwardly

FIG. 30.—ANGERS, LA TRINITÉ.

placed beneath it. The addition of an intermediate transverse arch and the conversion of the vault into sexpartite form restored the symmetry of piers, arches, and windows. In order, however, to obtain as much light as possible and to produce the effect of square nave bays, these intermediate transverse ribs were stilted and their imposts raised. Nor was this stilting confined to Anjou. It appears a number of times elsewhere often in churches where the ridge rib was not employed for example, in the cathedrals of Bremen and Limburg[197] in Germany, and in those of Ribe,[198] and Viborg in Denmark.[199]

[197] Lubke, I, p. 440, Fig. 313.
[198] Sturgis, II, p. 435, Fig. 382.
[199] Sturgis, II, p. 439, Fig. 386.

The church of the Certosa of Pavia in Italy (1396) has six-part vaults of similar type but presents a curious arrangement of square nave bays corresponding to rectangular bays in the side aisles (Plate I-d).[200]   The intermediate transverse arches, therefore, rise from corbels above the crowns of the side aisle arches, a fact which explains their higher imposts. Why such a vault should have been used can again be explained by the desire to obtain the best possible arrangement of windows.   Five-part vaults had already been used in the aisles of the Certosa to get square flanking chapels, and it was natural that the builders should have wished to have a clerestory window corresponding to each exterior bay of the church.   The fact that square nave and rectangular aisle bays were used at all would seem to have been due to the Italian fondness for this system which caused the least possible obstruction of the church interior by piers. The only curious feature is, therefore, the use of the six-part, instead of the more natural four-part, vault.

A somewhat similar arrangement with the substitution of two four-part vaults for the six-part vaults of Pavia is to be seen in the cathedral of Magdeburg,[201] where the same combination of nave and aisle bays occurs. The builders, like those of Pavia, first subdivided the outer longitudinal cells of the side aisle vaults by a half rib in order to obtain two windows instead of one, which would necessarily be of rather clumsy shape or of small size were it placed below the long, low wall rib of a simple rectangular four-part vault. Then to make the nave bays and clerestory windows correspond to those of the aisles in exterior elevation, as well as to obtain better window space, they constructed two rectangular four-part vaults over each square nave bay with their intermediate transverse rib resting on corbels above the aisle arches (Plate I-e).

EIGHT-PART VAULTING

There is one more important variant of the six-part vault which is especially interesting and unusual. It appears in the church of Saint Quiriace at Provins (Seine-et-Marne) (cir. 1160) (Fig. 31)[202] and con-

---

[200] See also one bay of Lincoln choir (Fig. 35) rebuilt cir. 1239, also Bourges, S. Pierre-le-Guillard, early thirteenth century, vaults rebuilt on original lines in the fifteenth century. Nesle (Somme) Ch. also has this vaulting form according to Moore, Mediaeval Church Architecture of England, p. 114, note 1.

[201] See also Erfurt, Frankiskanerkirche.

[202] Gurlitt, pl. 83.

sists in a division of the nave into great square bays each corresponding, not to two, but to three square bays in the side aisle (Plate I-f). The divisions thus formed are covered by what is really an eight-part vault, which is precisely like six-part vaulting except that there are three instead of two window cells in either side of each bay. Needless to say the immense size of the transverse triangular severies thus created presented a

FIG. 31.—PROVINS, SAINT QUIRIACE.

structural problem of much difficulty, and it is not surprising that such a vault was but seldom imitated,[203] particularly as the great discrepancy in the size of the vault cells and the awkward angles formed by their crowns give a decidedly unpleasant appearance. Nevertheless, there is one instance, at least, in which this system was not only imitated but transformed into a ten-part vault. This was at Boppart, Germany,[204] where the thirteenth century church has vaults with four window cells and but a single pair of diagonals. To break up the two remaining triangular severies, added surface ribs were introduced (Plate I-g).

Rectangular Nave Bays with Four-Part Cross-Ribbed Vaults

While the builders of Normandy were developing the sexpartite system just discussed, those of the Ile-de-France were experimenting with the simple four-part cross-ribbed vault of rectangular plan (Plate I-h). As in Normandy, the earliest churches of the province were in the main wooden roofed basilicas like the Basse-Oeuvre at Beauvais. When groined vaults first appeared in the Romanesque period, they were generally employed only in the side aisles, as at Morienval,[205] and if one may judge from these vaults, which have unfortunately been rebuilt, they were of slightly domed up section somewhat like those of Lombardy and the Rhenish provinces. Toward the beginning of the twelfth century, however, when the central power had been greatly strengthened under Louis VI. (1108-1137), there began a marked architectural advance which was destined to render this backward province the most important of all in the development of Gothic architecture. One of the earliest churches to mark this advance was Saint Étienne at Beauvais (probably early twelfth century) (Fig. 32), which, if one may judge from the form of the piers and the ribbed vault of the side aisles,[206] was planned from the foundation for vaulting throughout. Unfortunately the original vaults of the nave, if such existed, are no longer in position for they either gave way from lack of support, a natural supposition since they had no other abutment than the weight of the clerestory walls, or else they were so injured by the fire of 1180 that it was necessary to replace them by the existing vaults of the late twelfth century.

[203] Ex. Voulton (Seine-et-Marne), Ch. Baudot and Perrault-Dabot, I, pl. 62.
[204] Bumpus, illustration opp. p. 92.
[205] Ill. in Moore, p. 51.
[206] See p. 96 and Fig. 44.

These, while they do not make up for the loss of their predecessors, are nevertheless important because of their early date. They are antedated,

FIG. 32.—BEAUVAIS, SAINT ÉTIENNE.

however, by a number of very important churches which still retain, in part at least, their original vaulting.

IRREGULAR FOUR-PART VAULTING OF DURHAM CATHEDRAL

The first of these is the English cathedral of Durham. The date of its vaults is still the subject of a decided controversy, but whether they were built between 1093 and 1133 as Bond,[207] Rivoira,[208] and Moore[209] believe, or are later than those of Saint Denis, which is the claim of Lasteyrie,[210] they are of sufficiently early date to be important in a dis-

[207] Bond, p. 643.
[208] Rivoira, II, pp. 235-243.
[209] Moore, Mediaeval Church Architecture of England, p. 25.
[210] Lasteyrie, p. 497, note 1.

cussion of rectangular four-part vaulting. Those over the nave (Fig. 33) are especially interesting and furnish a unique variant of the standard type. It was the apparent intention of the builders to roof the nave with wood and for this purpose heavy transverse arches were constructed between the

FIG. 33.—DURHAM, CATHEDRAL.

alternate piers. When vaulting was determined upon, the nave was therefore already divided into square bays each containing two clerestory windows on a side. To vault these bays the builders might naturally have been expected to adopt the Lombard system of simple four-part vaults, but here in Durham, as in Saint Étienne at Caen, the impost level of the transverse arches was so low that a four-part vault would have made impossible the retention of the windows already in position above each nave arch. As these were absolutely essential in the north of England for lighting purposes, and also most important in preserving the symmetry of the bays, a change either in their size or position would have proved impractical. The six-part vault was the Norman method of solving a similar problem. But the builders of Durham invented a new system, made up of two rectangular cross-ribbed vaults in each bay, their intermediate supports afforded by corbels, and their alternate transverse arches omitted (Plate I-i). This omission of the intermediate rib gives a very unusual character to the vault but it preserves the alternate system with square nave bays so popular in Norman work, and at the same time has a great advantage over the six-part vault in that the transverse crown line of the window cells is perpendicular to the outer wall. The panels are therefore more symmetrical in elevation and the thrusts are more evenly distributed from pier to pier. The large central severy, however, afforded a difficult surface both for construction and support, and it is not surprising that the system was not repeated. As in the early ribbed vaults at Caen, wall ribs were not employed at Durham, and the abutment was provided only by flat pilasters and concealed flying buttresses, some of full and some of half arched form.[211]

Early Four-Part Ribbed Vaults in Normandy

That the rectangular four-part system of vaulting was developed in Normandy, as well as in England and the Ile-de-France, and very possibly independently of both, is proved by the early twelfth century abbey church of Lessay (Manche) (cir. 1130).[212] If the vaults of Lessay are an independent development it is hardly possible to see in them anything else than another effort to vault a church with square nave bays and yet provide the best possible vaulting to fit above the windows. A glance at the choir[213] will show that the alternate system was here employed just as in Saint Étienne at Caen, yet the builders introduced two four-part vaults instead of one of six-part type in each bay.[214] The transverse arches are still semicircular and the vault is somewhat rudimentary. The system as a whole may be considered as a fourth method[215] of the Norman builders to preserve their clerestory intact and still vault their churches. A slight advance is shown in the vaults at Pontorson (Manche) (middle of twelfth century). This is, however, a small church without side aisles and its vaults are in almost square bays with pointed transverse arches and considerably domed up at the crown. Wall ribs are still lacking as at Durham and Lessay.

[211] Bond, p. 370.
[212] Bond, pp. 315 and 319.
[213] Bond, p. 319.
[214] The system, moreover, is complete with a transverse arch which might seem to indicate that it was later than that at Durham.
[215] The other three are, the sexpartite and pseudo-sexpartite vaults and the irregular four-part method employed at Durham.

TRANSITIONAL FOUR-PART RIBBED VAULTS IN THE ILE-DE-FRANCE

The abbey church of Saint Germer-de-Fly (Oise) (cir. 1140), which still retains its original vaults in the choir and two eastern bays of the nave, presents another and perhaps more important example of rectangular four-part cross-ribbed vaulting. Its structural arches are of pointed section, and the piers and walls are strengthened by concealed flying-buttresses beneath the wooden roof of the triforium.[216] These are similar to those which have already been noted in La Trinité at Caen and in the nave of Durham,[217] but the vaults are superior in construction to those at Durham and are also provided with transverse arches between each rectangular bay. With the aid of this concealed buttress and the retention of the heavy Romanesque walls and small openings the vaults of Saint Germer were kept from falling, and it was doubtless this fact which led to the extension of the four-part system until it rivaled and at length became more popular than the six-part vaulting imported from Normandy and used at exactly the same period in the church of Saint Denis. A number of elementary features still remained at St. Germer, however. The transverse arches are but slightly pointed in section, the ribs are unusually heavy, and the diagonals of the choir bay are supported upon corbels[218] showing that the shaft arrangement was not yet in accord with the ribs to be carried.

A gradual development of the flying-buttress, and of the compound pier, a reduction in the size of the ribs,[219] and many other structural refinements rapidly followed one another in the period subsequent to the construction of Saint Germer and led to the perfection of rectangular four-part vaulting. The cathedral of Soissons (Aisne) (cir. 1212 on) (Fig. 67), for example, shows a considerable structural advance over Saint

[216] Moore, p. 80, Fig. 32.

[217] Whether these concealed butresses were first used in Normandy or the Ile-de-France is an open question, but in either case their origin would seem to be traceable to such prototypes as the ramping walls above the transverse aisle arches of such Lombard churches as Sant' Ambrogio at Milan and perhaps even to Roman monuments like the basilica of Maxentius at Rome. The really important question is to learn when these concealed buttresses were first raised above the aisle roofs to constitute true flying-buttresses. This would seem to have taken place in the Ile-de-France, perhaps at Domont as Porter suggests (Porter, II, pp. 91-92), or at Noyon towards the middle of the twelfth century.

[218] Ill. in Moore, p. 76.

[219] An example of the heavy ribs used in early work may be seen at Morienval, Fig. 77.

Germer. Its ribs are more decidedly pointed though still somewhat heavy and there is no hesitation in raising the impost of the vault far above the clerestory string-course, since its thrusts are easily met by exterior flying-buttresses.

DEVELOPED FOUR-PART RIBBED VAULTS

It is in the cathedral of Amiens (beg. 1218) (Fig. 69), however, that the four-part vault reaches its most daring if not its most perfect form. Here the builders constructed a vault similar to that of Soissons, but rising over one hundred and forty feet from the pavement. Its ribs are perfectly proportioned and finely moulded and the buttress system is completely developed. One awkward feature does, however, appear in the fact that the builders, perhaps, in order to concentrate the thrusts of the vaults upon the narrowest possible strip of outer wall, have made the wall intersection of the window severies follow an irregular curve which does not correspond to that of the wall rib in the portion from the impost to a point near the haunch. In spite of this defect, the cathedral of Amiens may well be considered as marking the highest development of rectangular ribbed vaulting. A study of other Gothic churches will disclose few, if any, improvements, either in appearance or construction, and many of the finest closely resemble this masterpiece.

THE CURVE OF VAULT RIBS

Such a study will, however, show a decided difference in the elevation of the transverse ribs and consequent shape of the vaults, which is worthy of some notice. If, for example, a triangle be inscribed beneath a number of these transverse arches, it will be found that the angles inside its base vary from about fifty degrees in Saint Germer-de-Fly, Rouen cathedral and Beverley Minster;[220] to fifty-five degrees in Soissons, Amiens, Salisbury, and Milan cathedrals, and Westminster Abbey; and even to sixty degrees in the cathedrals of Cologne and Reims. Moreover there is a great difference in the curve of these same transverse ribs. Those in Saint Germer, Beverley, and Rouen closely approach a semicircle, those in Amiens and Salisbury are much more pointed, but made up of two arcs

[220] These and the following churches are chosen at random merely for the purposes of comparison.

without, however, a long radius with the resulting flattened appearance to be noted at Cologne and Reims and more decidedly at Milan. All this would seem to indicate that the elevation of these ribbed vaults,—and this is true of six-part and complex vaults as well,—was largely a matter of individual taste with a tendency to favor the form used at Amiens. The reason for the employment of very sharp curves like those of Reims, Cologne and Milan, was doubtless due to the appreciation on the part of the builders of the fact that such curves greatly reduced the outward thrusts, rather than to any idea of beauty of appearance to be gained, for in this they are perhaps inferior to the less pointed examples.

Rectangular Four-Part Ribbed Vaults in Churches without Side Aisles

The use of rectangular four-part ribbed vaulting was not confined to churches with side aisles, but appears also in those with a single broad nave. It is the method employed in the Sainte Chapelle at Paris (fin. 1248), where there are simple salient buttresses, and there is a splendid example in the Cathedral of Albi (Tarn) (begun 1282) (Fig. 34), where the nave has a very wide span and is flanked by chapels in two stories between heavy pier buttresses which are thus enclosed in the church in a

Fig. 34.—Albi, Cathedral.

truly Byzantine manner. In the smaller church of Saint Nicholas at Toulouse these buttress chapels are in but one story and the bays are more nearly square in plan, a compromise between the square and rectangular systems which appears on an even larger scale in the cathedral of Saint Bertrand-des-Comminges (Haute-Garonne) (cir. 1304). As far as construction is concerned these vaults over a single broad nave offer no advance over those in churches with side aisles, not even requiring a scientific system of flying buttresses to offset their outward thrust. Their only importance lies in the very broad space sometimes covered by them.[221]

VAULTING WITH ADDED RIBS

The simple forms of ribbed vaulting just discussed were the ones most frequently in use during the best Gothic period. But among certain builders, there was a tendency even in the thirteenth century to introduce additional ribs into the vaults, a custom which later gave rise to a vast number of complicated vaulting systems especially in England, Spain and Germany. Even to enumerate these would be almost impossible and a description of each is out of the question, hence only those combinations which were frequently employed, or which gave rise to new types, will be discussed.

ORIGIN AND USE OF THE RIDGE RIB

Naturally enough the ridge rib was the first to be added to those already constituting the four-part vault (Plate I-j). But the vaults thus formed should be divided into two groups. The first most frequently found in France and already discussed in connection with the churches of Anjou,[222] is that in which the surface of each severy has a curved crown and the rib follows this curve, with the object, probably, both of subdividing the large rectangular bays, of marking with absolute exactness the crown line, and of aiding in rigidly fixing the central keystone, or even in the case of a six-part vault, of giving the same apparent division to the transverse severies as is found in those running longitudinally.

Though very similar to this first type, the second, which was developed and most used in England, is different, in that the ridge line is here per-

---

[221] For example in the cathedral of Albi, where the nave is sixty feet in width, and in that of Gerona (Spain), where it is over seventy.

[222] See pp. 49 and 70.

fectly horizontal, and the main purpose of the rib is to mark this horizontal line with absolute exactness and to give, what Bond terms a spine,[223] to the vault skeleton. In the earliest example in England, the transept aisle of Ripon cathedral (cir. 1170),[224] the ribs are so small as to be purely decorative. This leaves the choir of Lincoln cathedral (begun 1192) (Fig. 35) as the first English example of importance in which a

FIG. 35.—LINCOLN, CATHEDRAL.

true ridge rib appears. It is not yet absolutely horizontal since there is a slight curve to each severy. Its presence would seem to be due to the peculiar form of the vault, in which the ribs enclosing the window cells do not meet at a common point of intersection but at two points somewhat distant from each other along the ridge line where each pair is abutted by a single rib running to the nearest impost on the opposite wall (Plate I-1). This arrangement, which was probably planned to increase the amount of

[223] See Bond, p. 336.
[224] See Bond, p. 335.

centering in the large transverse panels and thus render their construction easier,[225] gives an extra keystone in each bay and it is quite possible that the ridge rib was introduced in order to unite these intersections and fix them in a straight line. It does not appear in the window cells where it would of course have been at an awkward angle with the outer walls.

Once introduced into English architecture the ridge rib was destined to play a most important part in its development. In the first place, it provided an easy method of assuring an absolutely level and straight ridge line and was thus especially welcome to English builders, who had been trained in the construction of vaults which were never more than slightly and often not at all domed up, and who were, besides, rather inferior masons, and not particularly skillful in making their masonry courses intersect in a perfect manner. In the second place, it furnished admirable abutment for tiercerons or intermediate ribs,[226] which were perhaps suggested by such a vault as Lincoln choir as being valuable additions to the rib skeleton and were thereafter very generally used to provide more permanent centering and to further reduce the size of the vault panels.

It is, however, notable that a longitudinal ridge rib appears added to simple four-part vaults without the introduction of tiercerons or transverse ridge ribs at a comparatively early date in Worcester cathedral choir (after 1224),[227] Westminster Abbey choir (1245-1260), and Gloucester cathedral nave (1245), and that it is used in France in a number of churches where there are no tiercerons.[228] In such cases it serves the primary purpose of clearly marking the ridge line, which is especially difficult to adjust in vaults with level crowns. That it was the longitudinal effect thus produced which was desired is evidenced by the fact that except when there were tiercerons in the longitudinal cells, the transverse ridge rib was rarely added to such vaults (Plate I-k). Among the very few examples are the cathedral of Tulle (Corrèze) (twelfth century) and the fifteenth century chapel of the château at Blois, both of them in France.[229]

---

[225] See Bond, p. 336.

[226] As a matter of fact these in their turn help to support the ridge rib.

[227] See Street, p. 78 for a drawing (from Wilde) of this vault before its restoration.

[228] See p. 93 for examples.

[229] So far as the writer knows there are no examples of the simple transverse ridge rib in England, where one would naturally expect to find it used.

TIERCERON VAULTING

The introduction of a ridge rib was only the first step in the development of multiple rib vaulting. It was not long before the builders, especially in England, began to add intermediate ribs or tiercerons between the transverse arches and the diagonals. These may possibly have been inspired by the extra ribs in the choir of Lincoln cathedral (Fig. 35 and Plate I-l), but whatever their origin they became a common feature of later Gothic and gave rise to what may be termed tierceron vaulting. In the transverse vault severies, which in England were really sections of a tunnel vault because of the level crown line, these ribs acted largely as added centering and as decorative features. But when used in the window cells they served another purpose as well for they enabled the builders to convert the ordinary "ploughshare" curve of the vaulting conoid into a series of flat panels which could be constructed with much less difficulty as far as the laying of the masonry courses was concerned.

Sometimes the tiercerons are used in both the transverse and the longitudinal severies and sometimes only in one of them. Their number also varies greatly, though of course they are always in pairs. Lincoln cathedral presbytery (cir. 1266-1280) (Fig. 36) affords an example of a single pair in each of the large transverse severies with none in the window cells (Plate I-m), while Chester cathedral chapter-house (first half of the thirteenth century), and Worcester cathedral nave (cir. 1350-1377) (Fig. 89) are rare examples of the opposite arrangement (Plate I-n).[230] To support such tiercerons as these at their crown, a transverse ridge rib was added to the construction, sometimes as in Chester chapter-house (Plate I-n), Lincoln nave (before 1233),[231] and Ely presbytery (1235-1252),[232] running out only to the new keystone (Plate I-o) and thus playing a purely structural rôle, but often extending to the window head (Plate I-p) as in Lichfield cathedral south transept (cir. 1220) and choir (fourteenth century). These portions of Lichfield, together with the nave of Lincoln and the presbytery of Ely cathedral, are also important as showing the employ-

---

[230] Moreover the tiercerons at Worcester would seem to have been an afterthought. See Moore, Mediaeval Church Architecture of England, p. 175.

[231] Illustrated in Bond, p. 327.

[232] Illustrated in Bond, p. 327. See also Lichfield' Cath. nave for similar transverse rib.

ment of a single pair of tiercerons in each of the four panels of the vaulting bays (Plate I-p). This system is slightly varied in the naves of Lichfield and Hereford (Plate I-q-r), where the true transverse arch is omitted between the bays, but these vaults like those of Durham are merely variants of the more standard types.[233]

FIG. 36.—LINCOLN, CATHEDRAL.

The introduction of a single pair of tiercerons in each major panel was soon followed, especially in the window cells where the surface was warped, by the use of two (Plate I-s) and even of three such pairs (Plate I-t). Two are found in Hereford cathedral south transept (cir. 1400),[234] and in the choir of Saint Mary Redcliffe at Bristol (fifteenth century),[235] while three appear at Exeter (between 1280-1350) (Fig. 37). This last

[233] Not without their influence, however, as a number of late churches could be cited in which there is no true transverse rib, as for example the minster at Berne (Switzerland), (illustrated in Michel, III, p. 52, Fig. 31).

[234] See Bond, p. 333.

[235] Dehio and von Bezold, II, p. 234, Fig. 1.

may well be said to mark the highest point in tierceron vaulting,[236] and it must be acknowledged that the decorative effect produced is most pleasing. Placed as they are over comparatively low naves, these vaults harmonize in an admirable manner with the clustered piers, moulded archivolts, and

FIG. 37.—EXETER, CATHEDRAL.

substantial walls provided for their support, and carry to the crown of the vault that wealth of moulding which lends so much of grace and charm to the English Gothic of the Decorated period. Were such vaults used above the lofty naves of Amiens or Beauvais, they would doubtless appear oppressively heavy but the lowness and solidity of English construction entirely dispels such a feeling. Of course, tiercerons are not essential members of the vaulting system and perhaps they were better omitted altogether, but that their usage can be vindicated from an aesthetic standpoint is proved by such vaults as those at Exeter.

[236] A larger number of tiercerons is frequently found but not in vaults without liernes, except in very rare instances such as Oxford Schools Tower, where there are three pairs of tiercerons in each severy. Plan in Bond, p. 324-8.

Lierne Vaulting

Tierceron vaulting did not, however, mark the limit to which the English Gothic builders were to carry their passion for added ribs and complex design, and it was not long before short connecting ribs known as liernes were added to the tierceron vaults. These may have been introduced by the builders from a feeling that the tiercerons did not have sufficient abutment, as Bond suggests,[237] but it is more reasonable to suppose that they are the result of a striving for still more complex vaulting forms and still more decorative patterns in vault construction.

The combinations in lierne vaulting are of course without number and only a few can be discussed. The simplest is that known as the star vault (Plate I-u) in which there is a single pair of tiercerons in each of the four main vault panels with short liernes connecting the points of their intersection with the ridge ribs, with a point in the same plane on each of the diagonals. A simple example occurs at Oxford in the Proscholium[238] and one of the same general type but much elaborated, in the choir of Oxford cathedral.[239]

It is almost impossible to classify the remaining lierne vaults under separate heads, though there are certain characteristics which belong to one group and not to another. For example, some, like those of the nave of Saint Mary Redcliffe at Bristol[240] have no ridge rib, others have a single rib like that found in tierceron vaulting. These last might again be classified according to the number and arrangement of their liernes. Thus in Ely cathedral choir[241] (beg. 1322) and Norwich nave (vaults cir. 1470)[242] there are but few liernes, while in Winchester cathedral nave (cir. 1394-1460) there is a much larger number. Still other lierne vaults have more than one ridge rib. Of these, the choir (1337-1357), and Lady chapel of Gloucester cathedral (cir. 1457-1489), and the nave of Tewkesbury Abbey (Fig. 38)[243] are representative and varied examples. All have three ridge ribs which is the standard number.

[237] Bond, p. 340.
[238] Illustrated in Bond, p. 329.
[239] Illustrated in Bond, p. 331.
[240] Michel, III, p. 27, Fig. 17.
[241] Illustrated in Bond, p. 329.
[242] Illustrated in Bond, p. 330.
[243] See also illustration in Bond, p. 332.

INTERPENETRATING MULTIPLE RIBBED VAULTS

In these last three churches, however, as well as in Winchester nave and in numerous other examples not cited, there is a still more decided change in the form of the vault than that brought about by the use of liernes or added ridge ribs. This lies in the fact that the window cells no longer rise to the full height of the vault, so that the entire system is

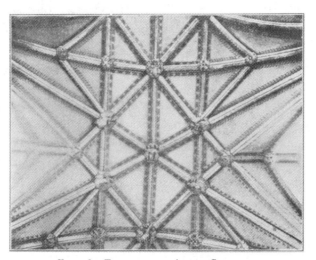

FIG. 38.—TEWKESBURY, ABBEY CHURCH.

practically a reversion to the Romanesque tunnel vault pierced on either side with lunettes, in other words, to the interpenetrating vault. The ribs merely form a permanent centering, and generally no attempt is made to concentrate the pressure on a narrow strip of wall,[244] or to make use of flying-buttresses.[245] Except for the decoration which they afford, the ribs have little structural value though they do make possible lighter masonry in the web than would be possible in a continuous tunnel vault.

The height of the window cells in such vaults was not at all fixed though it was quite frequently determined by the intersection of two ribs running diagonally from each side of the window to the second impost

[244] See illustration of Gloucester choir in Bond, p. 334.
[245] See illustration in Bond, opp. p. 132.

on the opposite wall of the church.[246] Such window cells as these naturally left a large central space along the crown of the vault, which was usually decorated by extra lierne and ridge ribs.

TRACERY VAULTS

Not content with the liernes as a decoration, an innovation appears in Tewkesbury choir,[247] Saint George's Chapel at Windsor[248] and elsewhere, which consists in the application of raised mouldings forming tracery patterns on the few open spaces left between the ribs of complex lierne vaults. It is as if the tracery of a window were applied to a background of stone, with ribs taking the place of mullions. The patterns are usually trefoils or quatrefoils, but other forms, as, for example, the cross shaped flowers in the fan vaults at Peterborough (Fig. 39) also occur.

The natural consequence of such added mouldings and ribs as those just described was to bring about the total sacrifice of the structural principles of ribbed vaulting to those which were purely decorative, and it is not surprising that such a vault as that of the choir of Wells cathedral (1329-1363),[249] in which the ribs have but the slightest claim to structural purpose should be found even at its early date as an example of this decadent stage in English vaulting.

FAN VAULTING

But the addition of multiple ribs lead not only to such debased vaulting as that at Wells. It must have played a large part in the creation of the distinctly novel construction known as fan vaulting. For in a vault with many tiercerons, as for example, that at Exeter (Fig. 37), or Hereford south transept,[250] the combined surfaces between the ribs is a cross between half of a hollow sided pyramid and a cone. This is true because, like most of the English churches, the wall rib is not highly stilted to concentrate pressures on a narrow strip of outer wall, or to leave a more pointed window head as in France, but it and the tiercerons and diagonals have much the same curvature. It was natural, therefore, that the English

---

[246] See illustration of Tewkesbury nave, Wells choir (Bond, p. 332) and Gloucester choir (Bond, p. 334).
[247] Illustrated in Bond, p. 330.
[248] Illustrated in Bond, p. 332.
[249] Illustrated in Bond, p. 332.
[250] Illustrated in Bond, p. 333.

builders should have conceived the idea of making all the ribs of just the same curvature but of different length according to their several positions. This they did in Sherborne Abbey nave (vaulted 1475-1504).[251] Here the builders very logically used the shortest rib as a measure and connected

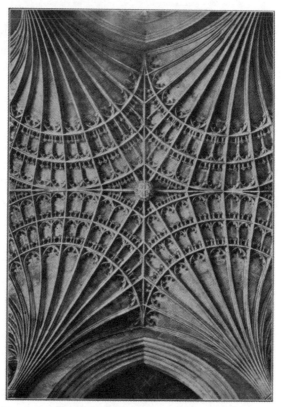

FIG. 39.—PETERBOROUGH, CATHEDRAL.

the points at corresponding distances from the imposts on each rib with liernes. A central space was thus left, which at Sherborne was covered by prolonging a number of the radiants and adding a tracery of liernes and mouldings. The vault as thus constituted is not yet of pure fan type. It was first necessary to replace the ring of straight liernes by those of curved plan and to add one ring above another at the various points of intersection of the tiercerons and transverse ridge ribs, until practically the entire space to the vault crown was filled. Thus, in certain of the

[251] Illustrated in Bond, p. 333.

fan vaults of Peterborough (second half of the fifteenth century) (Fig. 39), there are three such rings leaving but a small diamond shaped central space which is largely filled by the keystone of the bay.[252] Others down the side aisles where the bays are smaller have but a single ring and a much larger central space. In vaults of the Peterborough type, the radiants are continued through this central panel in a decorative way, but in the cloister at Gloucester (before 1412) (Fig. 40), this portion of the

FIG. 40.—GLOUCESTER, CATHEDRAL, CLOISTER.

vault is left entirely flat and decorated with tracery patterns in raised mouldings such as are usually found in window heads. The conoids, also, are covered with tracery rather than continuous ribs and the term "Fan-Tracery Vaults" might properly be used to distinguish them from the more common type.[253]

In the matter of construction, fan vaulting differs from any preceding

[252] See also Cambridge, King's College chapel, illustrated in Bond, p. 333.
[253] See also Oxford, Christ Church staircase, illustrated in Bond, p. 348.

method. Its ribs are all of precisely the same curvature, their length being determined by the position which they occupy, and they are no longer supporting but rather decorative members. The lower portions of some of the vaults still resemble true ribbed vaulting in that the tas-de-charge is used, and also in the fact that the ribs still rise in a single long voussoir from their imposts to the first horizontal ring. But from this point to the crown, the ribs and mouldings are merely carved in relief upon the jointed masonry, which they therefore in no way support. In some fan vaults, as, for example, in Islip's chapel in Westminster Abbey,[254] and in Gloucester cathedral cloister (Fig. 40), the rib is even carved upon the vault masonry for its entire length.

The one structural advantage which the fan vault afforded lay in the fact that it could be built up of practically horizontal courses in a manner to exert very little outward thrust; while the substitution of curved, for straight liernes did away with the awkward angular intersections characteristic of lierne vaulting. Altogether, it is both a clever and beautiful type of vaulting well suited to the builders of the Perpendicular Gothic period, with their fondness for intricate decorative rather than structural problems.

Pendants

Because of its late development, fan vaulting was not extensively used to cover an entire church. Nevertheless, King's College Chapel at Cambridge (vaulted between 1512 and 1515),[255] and Bath Abbey (cir. 1500-1540),[256] furnish two excellent examples, to which might be added Henry VII's Chapel at Westminster (cir. 1500-1520).[257] The latter is essentially of fan type, though the fans are in combination with a system of transverse arches and pendants best understood from the photograph and drawing just cited. The vaults in the foregoing churches, do however exhibit minor differences. For example, the transverse arches are practically concealed in the vaults of the naves at Sherborne, and Bath and in the east aisle of Peterborough, while they are prominent in Henry VII's and King's College chapels. Moreover, in a number of fan vaults as well

[254] Illustrated in Willis, p. 50.
[255] Illustrated in Bond, p. 333.
[256] The vaults are modern but the church was planned to have this type.
[257] Illustrated in Bond, opp. p. 348, also Willis, pl. III, opp. p. 54.

as in others of different type, pendant voussoirs or keystones are employed. These are supported by some clever building trick and beautifully carved either as lanterns or reliquaries,—like those of Oxford cathedral choir,[258]—or decorated with rich floral, heraldic, or other designs. Thus they play a rôle which is largely decorative, though one which also marks a very clever building technique.[259]

Vaults with Added Ribs—Outside of England

The vaults thus far discussed have been largely those of England, but some of the types with added ribs, most highly developed in that country were not without Continental examples. In France, for instance, ridge ribs, besides being used in vaults of the domed up Anjou type already described, are also found marking level ridges like those of the standard English vaults. The nave of the abbey church of Souvigny (Allier) (late fifteenth century), the north transept of the cathedral of LeMans (before 1430), and the chapel of the Maison de Jacques Coeur at Bourges (middle of fifteenth century) afford excellent examples of the use of the longitudinal without the transverse ridge rib, while the chapel of the château of Blois, and the cathedral of Tulle (Corrèze), have already been cited as rare instances in which both were employed in vaults with level crowns. That the French builders were even more impressed with the decorative possibilities which these ribs afforded than were those of England is perhaps shown by the fact that, whereas in England this rib has carved decoration[260] only rarely as in the nave of Lichfield cathedral it is carved in no less than three of the French examples cited, the chief among these being Souvigny, in which a deeply cut foliate design decorates both sides of the rib throughout its entire length. In Spain also there is a notable example of the decoration of both a longitudinal and transverse ridge rib in the form of a knotted rope or scourge in the cathedral of Vizeu.[261]

Tiercerons as well as ridge ribs were freely used on the continent

---

[258] Illustrated in Bond, p. 297. See also Oxford, Divinity School, illustrated in Bond, p. 331 and Henry VII's Chapel, illustrated in Bond, opp. p. 348.

[259] For an extended discussion of English vaulting see Bond, English Church Architecture, Vol. I, Chap. V, pp. 279-384.

[260] The diagonals of many vaults in France and Spain and especially in England had been decorated with carving, particularly in the early Gothic period.

[261] Illustrated in Michel, IV, p. 858.

though usually not at a very early date. Fine examples are to be seen in France in such churches as those of Brou (Ain) (1506-1536), and Saint Nicolas-du-Port (Meurthe-et-Moselle) (cir. 1505).[262] Both of these are also of interest because their vaults still retain the domed up crown characteristic of French construction, and because of this the builders, to avoid the awkward rise and fall of continuous ridge ribs, have brought these out only far enough to meet the pair of tiercerons in each severy. Many other examples of tierceron vaulting could be cited both in France and elsewhere, but they would add nothing of importance from a structural standpoint.

As for lierne vaults, they, too, appear on the Continent especially in Germany and Spain. The choir of Freiburg cathedral (second half of fifteenth century) (Fig. 72), and the church of the Holy Cross at Gmund,[263] show two German types, both of which resemble English vaults which have already been discussed. In Spain, the new cathedral at Salamanca[264] (begun 1513), the cathedral at Segovia (begun 1525),[265] and many other churches might be cited, while in France the church of Mézières (begun 1499),[266] and in Switzerland the cathedral of Bern (cir. 1421-1598)[267] show the extent of the style, sometimes with sharply defined domed up bays as in Mézières and sometimes a continuous vault like that of Bern. Finally in some instances, as, for example, the Stadtkirche of Wimpfen[268] the liernes are curved giving a still more complicated character to the vault.

Fan vaulting was unused[269] outside of Great Britain, but there are many instances of the employment of extensively decorated vaults, including those with pendants of somewhat English character. Among the latter are Saint Pierre at Caen and Saint Eustache at Paris (1532-1637),[270] while pendants of especially exaggerated type are to be seen in the vault of one of the chapels off the south side aisle of Noyon cathe-

---

[262] Enlart, I, Fig. 318, opp. p. 558.
[263] Lubke, I, p. 540, Fig. 373. See also Freiberg-i-Sachsen, Cath. (Hartung, I, pl. 5).
[264] Plan in Street, pl. IV, opp. p. 104.
[265] Plan in Street, pl. XII, opp. p. 194.
[266] Michel, III, p. 10, Fig. 4.
[267] Michel, III, p. 52, Fig. 31.
[268] Hartung, II, pl. 114.
[269] So far as the writer is aware.
[270] Michel, IV, p. 567, Fig. 376.

dral (Fig. 41). A tendency to decorate the panels is also noticeable in a number of late French vaults, as for example that of the chapel of Saint Jacques at Cléry (Loiret) (probably after 1485) (Fig. 42), where each of the larger divisions of a complicated lierne and tierceron vault is deco-

FIG. 41.—NOYON, CATHEDRAL, CHAPEL.

rated by a wallet and staff or a scourge in low relief. At Rue (Somme), in the chapel of Saint Esprit,[271] there is a somewhat similar vault with heraldic devices and floral ornament on the panels. But even more notable are the angels in the round which have been added for decorative purposes in four of the severies of the vaults in one bay of the side aisle of the north transept (sixteenth century) in Senlis (Oise) cathedral (Fig. 43). The final stage in elaborate vaulting, is perhaps, to be seen in such a vault as that of the Chapelle de la Vièrge at La Ferté-Bernard (Sarthe)[272] which dates from 1535-1544. Here the panels are merely portions of a

[271] Enlart, I, pp. 598-599, Fig. 323.
[272] Enlart, I, pp. 676-677, Fig. 345. See also Bristol cathedral, Berkeley Chapel (cir. 1340) illustrated in Bond, p. 329.

flat ceiling resting upon a series of arches arranged like ribs, but carrying a tracery framework upon which the elaborately decorated ceiling with its mouldings and stalactite pendants is made to rest.

Side Aisle Vaulting

There now remain for consideration before closing this chapter, the ribbed vaults of the aisles and triforia of Gothic churches. Very naturally the general development of ribbed vaulting in the aisles closely paral-

Fig. 42.—Cléry, Chapel of Saint Jacques.

lels that in the nave. In by far the larger number of churches, the side aisle bays are square and covered with simple four-part cross-ribbed vaults. As in the case of the nave, those of early date have many clumsy features. Thus in the aisles of Saint Étienne at Beauvais (Fig. 44)—which, fortunately, retain a few bays of their primitive vaults dating from about 1125 —the diagonals are heavy (cir. 20-25 cm. thick)[273] and either square with simple bevelled edges or of single torus section. No wall rib is found and the transverse arches, besides being very thick, are of round-headed form, highly stilted to bring them up to approximately the general vault level. The vault itself is slightly domed up at the crown and besides the primi-

[273] See Dehio and von Bezold, II, p. 82.

FIG. 43.—SENLIS, CATHEDRAL, CHAPEL VAULT.

FIG. 44.—BEAUVAIS, SAINT ÉTIENNE.

tive characteristics just enumerated, its panels are composed of small stones roughly joined and in very uneven courses, while the ribs themselves are built up of short voussoirs, which are not combined at their springing in the familiar tas-de-charge of more developed Gothic work. The cathedral of Sens presents in its side aisles (Fig. 45), which date from the twelfth century[274] a slightly different system. The transverse

FIG. 45.—SENS, CATHEDRAL.

arches are still heavy and semicircular but they are not stilted. The diagonals rise from corner corbels—a fact which may prove that the aisles were originally planned for groined vaulting and thus no provision made for the cross-ribs,—and they are also semicircular, thus giving the vault a decidedly domed up character. This makes these vaults at Sens very similar to Lombard work and it would seem as though their builders

[274] Perhaps as early as between 1124-1140 when there was a reconstruction of the cathedral. The character of their construction certainly would not be inconsistent with such a date.

had the same object of saving centering by the use of ribs as obtained in Lombardy. There is one apparent advance over those at Beauvais in the presence of a wall rib, but this is of too wide a span to fit under its severy, and it would seem to have been designed to mark the wall intersection of groined rather than ribbed vaulting.

The early aisle vaults in England are generally similar to those at Beauvais, with even less doming or none at all. The earliest would seem to be those in Peterborough, Durham and the north nave aisle of Gloucester cathedrals, all dating, apparently, from before 1140. Although similar to those in Saint Étienne at Beauvais they differ in the comparative lowness of their transverse arches, which are but slightly stilted, and in the correspondingly reduced curve of the diagonals, which are less than semicircles and thus do not raise the crown of the vault. The explanation of this may very possibly be found in the desire of the builders to avoid cutting into the level of the triforium floor, especially at Peterborough, where this is a true gallery, and also in their familiarity with the flat crowned groined vault, which they had previously used in crypts and elsewhere. The form of the diagonals is in any case displeasing, as they spring from the shafts at an awkward angle and, furthermore, render the thrusts of the vault excessive.[275]

Many structural refinements were, of course, necessary before these crude vaults gave rise to the fully developed type, but these refinements followed in general the same order as those in the larger nave vaults. First came the introduction of the pointed arch and its use for the transverse and longitudinal ribs in place of the semicircular type. This change may be seen in such early vaults as those of Noyon cathedral (cir. 1150) where pointed arches are used throughout. The noticeable feature here is the great size of the transverse ribs compared to that of the diagonals. This same feature continues to appear in a gradually lessening degree in many of the churches of the transitional period, and even in the developed Gothic of the thirteenth century, as, for example, in Bourges and Amiens cathedrals. This may, perhaps, be explained by the function of this transverse arch which was not merely a centering for the

[275] Ribs rising in a somewhat similar manner are to be found in the south of France, in the crypt of the church of Saint Gilles (Gard.) (Ill. in Lasteyrie, p. 263, Fig. 253) or the chapel of the Pont Saint-Benezet at Avignon (Vaucluse), where they mark the intersection of two flattened tunnel vaults.

vault panel, but carried a considerable amount of the weight of the exterior buttress piers and wall pilasters which were connected above the aisle roofs by the arch of the flying buttress. These heavy transverse ribs also aided materially in bracing the nave piers and tying them to the outer walls. Sometimes, as in the beautiful aisles of Rouen cathedral, all the ribs are of the same section, but whether they were all the same or not, such vaults as those at Rouen and Amiens set the standard for developed Gothic side aisles.

Five-Part Aisle Vaults

Other methods, however, were employed. Perhaps the chief among these is the five-part vault, in which the triangular severy nearest the outer wall in a four-part vault is subdivided by a half rib running to the main vault crown (Fig. 46). The advantage of such a system lies in the

Fig. 46.—Beauvais, Cathedral, five-part vault.

fact that it permits a more pleasing arrangement of windows in the outer wall, especially in bays of rectangular plan, like those in the Certosa at Pavia and Magdeburg cathedral already discussed, where the windows would otherwise fit but awkwardly beneath the broad low wall rib. The same system was also used in aisles with practically square bays, as, for example, in the cathedral of Coutances (Fig. 82), in Saint Urbain at Troyes and in many English churches.[276] Here, too, the explanation is to be found in the window arrangement, especially in the English and Norman Gothic examples, where these windows are of the slender lancet type, which could not be satisfactorily placed beneath the comparatively low wall rib of a square four-part vault.

MULTIPLE-RIBBED AISLE VAULTS

With the introduction of ridge ribs, tiercerons, and liernes, the side aisles show the same changes as those which took place in the nave. Simple ridge ribs appear, for example, in Lichfield cathedral, liernes at Worcester, while tierceron vaults could be cited in great number. Fan vaults, too, were used in the aisles, and have already been discussed in connection with those of the nave. Reconstructions sometimes produced an unusual vaulting system like that of Beauvais cathedral (cir. 1284), where transverse arches with tracery spandrels were added across each original aisle bay, giving the vault a pseudo-sexpartite character. True six-part vaulting was by its very nature ill-suited for use in the aisles and is very rarely found. There is an example, however, in Magdeburg cathedral.[277] A desire for novelty also seems to have been the cause of unusual vaults, such as those of Bristol cathedral choir aisles,[278] in which low transverse tracery arches separate the bays and carry a system of ribs which subdivide each bay into two rectangular four-part vaults running lengthwise of the aisle.

TRIFORIUM VAULTING

Although similar in plan to the side aisles, the triforia were apt to be a little later in being given ribbed vaults. In the abbey church of Saint Germer-de-Fly (Oise) (cir. 1140) and in the choir of La Madeleine at Vézelay (Yonne) (cir. 1160 or 1170), for example, the triforium is not only left with groined vaults but is also constructed with round-headed arches, although both the ribbed vault and pointed arch are used in the aisles. This peculiarity may be due to the fact that groined vaults were

---

[276] Lincoln, Cath. nave aisle. Plan in Bond, pp. 308-9; Salisbury, Cath.; Southwell, Minster.

[277] Hartung, I, pl. 16.

[278] Illustrated in Bond, p. 329.

easier and cheaper to construct over a low space like the gallery than a ribbed vault would have been, because they involved less careful stone cutting than was required for the ribs.   Moreover, since the chief object of the transitional builders in using the ribbed vault would seem to have been to save centering, their object would not have been especially well served in the triforia, which were kept low to avoid detracting from the clerestory and therefore required but little centering compared to that which would have been needed for groined vaults in the side aisles.   Another system with possibly a similar reason for its use appears in Mantes (Seine-et-Oise) cathedral (end of twelfth century), where the aisles are ribbed and surmounted by a triforium with transverse tunnel vaults, a most exceptional arrangement.

It was only when the triforium began to play a larger rôle in the church plan, when it was perhaps used for congregational purposes, that its vaulting began to develop like that of the aisles.   Thus in the cathedral of Senlis (Oise) (cir. 1150) (Fig. 47), the triforium though comparatively

FIG. 47.—SENLIS, CATHEDRAL.

low, is a veritable second story above the side aisles with its own good sized windows. Its vaults are still of rather primitive ribbed type. The transverse arches, though pointed, are heavy, and to avoid the flattened curve which the diagonals would otherwise have, the vault is given a domed up crown. The cathedral of Laon (Aisne) (cir. 1170) (Fig. 48)

FIG. 48.—LAON, CATHEDRAL.

possesses a triforium of slightly greater height but still retaining excessively heavy ribs and domed up vaults. The triforia of the naves of Noyon (Oise) cathedral (cir. 1150-1180) and of Notre Dame at Chalons-sur-Marne (Marne) (1157-1183) show a gradual reduction in the size of these ribs, all of which finally become of practically equal section in the triforium of the cathedral of Notre Dame at Paris (beg. 1163), where the doming up of the crown also disappears to a large extent and where the gallery itself is nearly as lofty as the side aisles. After the beginning of the thirteenth century, triforia rapidly decline in popularity and are but rarely found except in Normandy, where there are beautiful examples in such churches as Saint Étienne at Caen choir rebuilt in the first quarter of the thirteenth century. Owing to its early decline in popularity, the triforium never presents those complex vaulting systems of the late Gothic period which have been described as appearing in the nave and aisles.

NAVE AND AISLES OF EQUAL HEIGHT

In closing this chapter brief mention should be made of the series of churches in which the aisle vaults are nearly or quite as high as those of the nave, which they therefore aid in supporting. Among the numerous examples of such churches, the cathedral of Poitiers (Vienne) (cir. 1160 and thirteenth century) illustrates the type in which the vaults of the aisles are slightly lower than those of the nave, while Saint Serge at Angers has all the vaults at exactly the same level. Both are of Anjou type but this is due only to their geographical situation, for the system was widely extended.[279] In Germany there is a fine early example in Saint Elizabeth at Marburg (cir. 1235),[280] with vaulting of simple Gothic character, while the church of the Holy Cross at Gmund[281] is covered with vaulting of complex lierne type. Except for the change in interior elevation which the system brought about and the fact that it removed the necessity for flying-buttresses, it did not show any special progress along structural lines. It must be acknowledged that the churches thus constructed possess a most pleasing effect of spaciousness in their interior elevation, though this is offset by the lack of direct light in the nave. A final example of a church similar to those mentioned above but with a new vaulting system is afforded by Saint Florentin at Amboise (Indre-et-Loire) (fifteenth-sixteenth century). Its aisles are very narrow and are covered by transverse tunnel vaults in much the same manner as a number of Romanesque churches already discussed, except that the nave is here roofed with a ribbed vault. It is but a variant of the standard vaulting types described in this chapter.

[279] Examples include: Linköping, Cath.; Paderborn, Cath.; Minden, Cath.; Mainz, S. Stephen; Landshut, Saint Martin; Prenzlau, Marienkirche; Heidelberg, Peterskirche; Paris. Sainte Chapelle (lower church); Chaumont, Ch.; Perugia, Cath.; Winchester, Cath. (Lady chapel); Belem (Portugal) Ab. Ch.; Barcelona, Cath.; Freiberg-i-Sachsen, Cath. (1494-1501); Hartung, I, pl. 5; Soest, Sta Maria zur Wiese, Hartung, I, pl. 49; Stendal, S. Maria (cir. 1450), Hartung, II, pl. 69.
[280] Hartung, III, pl. 126.
[281] Illustration in Lubke, I, p. 540, Fig. 373.

CHAPTER II

TRANSEPT AND CROSSING VAULTS

Transepts with Tunnel Vaults

Because of the close resemblance in plan and structure between them, the transept was vaulted like the nave in by far the larger number of instances. Thus in the Romanesque schools, where the nave was tunnel vaulted, similar vaults were generally placed above the transept as well. They were, moreover, well suited to this position, especially where there were no transept aisles, for the outer walls running down to the ground afforded them excellent support and also provided space for windows of considerable size. It is not surprising, therefore, to find the tunnel-vaulted transept the standard in Romanesque church architecture, an example appearing even as far north as Jedburgh Abbey in Scotland, although this was a church of the Norman school in which the nave was probably originally roofed with wood.[1] Even in the school of Perigord, where the naves are domed, the transept is frequently covered with a tunnel vault as, for example, in the churches of Souillac (Lot), Tremolac (Dordogne), and Vieux Mareuil (Dordogne), in the cathedral of Angoulême, and perhaps originally in the cathedral of Saint Front at Perigueux.[2] Occasionally, however, other forms displace the tunnel vault in transept construction.

One of these appears in the abbey church of Cluny (Saône-et-Loire) (early twelfth century). Here the bays of the transept, corresponding to the side aisles of the church are tunnel vaulted, but beyond these, there are two projecting bays, the inner one square and covered by an octagonal dome on trumpet squinches, the outer covered with a tunnel vault at a lower level[3] than that over the two bays adjoining the crossing. Above the dome

---

[1] See Butler, p. 78.
[2] See Lasteyrie, p. 480 and notes 1-2.
[3] From its elevation, this would seem to have been added later.

rises an octagonal tower and spire, and the whole composition of this bay shows that it was intended to be a flanking tower like those to be seen at Angoulême, Tréguier (Côtes-du-Nord), and Exeter cathedrals. For such a tower, a dome is more suitable than a tunnel vault, because it exerts less outward thrust. This is also better distributed.

A more original method of transept vaulting is to be seen in certain churches of the school of Auvergne, among them Notre Dame-du-Port at Clermont-Ferrand (Puy-de-Dôme) (eleventh and twelfth century) (Figs. 49, 50) and Saint Étienne at Nevers (Nièvre) (cir. 1097).[4] Here each

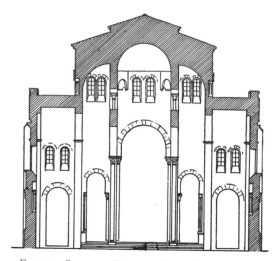

FIG. 49.—CLERMONT-FERRAND, NOTRE DAME-DU-PORT.

arm of the transept is divided into two distinct vaulting bays by a transverse arch continuing the line of the outer wall of the church. All the projecting portion is then covered by a tunnel vault, while that bay which corresponds to a continuation of the side aisles is covered by a half tunnel vault, its axis at right angles to the transept proper and rising from above the crown of the intermediate transverse arch to the springing of the crossing dome (Figs. 49-50). Such a vault has much to commend it, for it is most logical in affording excellent abutment for the dome, and at the same time it receives abutment from the tunnel vault of the outer transept bay. Curiously enough, one church of the school, namely that at

[4] Other examples include: Issoire, Saint Paul, and the churches at Saint Saturnin and Saint Nectaire (Puy-de-Dôme).

Orcival (Puy-de-Dôme) (twelfth century),[5] while following the main lines laid down by the vaults just described, differs from them in having full tunnel vaults instead of half tunnels abutting the dome. This is a less

Fig. 50.—Clermont-Ferrand, Notre Dame-du-Port.

satisfactory form in that these vault have to be excessively high in order to bring their thrusts to the proper level, but they do possess the advantage of providing excellent window space above the transept roofs.

Transepts with Ribbed Vaulting
Five-Part Ribbed Vaults

With the introduction of ribbed vaulting, examples of six-part vaults, four-part vaults of rectangular and square plan and many forms of complicated vaulting are to be found in the transept exactly as they have been in the nave. Only those vaults which are unusual in character will therefore be discussed. Of these the most important is the five-part rectangular vault sometimes used as a termination of the transept arm. From its appearance in Normandy, and its evident relation to sexpartite vaulting, this method may be assumed to have arisen there. The Abbaye-aux-Dames

[5] Illustrated in Lasteyrie, p. 445, Fig. 463.

at Caen (early twelfth century) affords an example of such a vault. It was evidently employed to subdivide the end walls into bays similar to those in the remainder of the church, and thus provide a uniform elevation and window arrangement throughout the edifice. In spite of its uniformity the arrangement is an awkward one, for it brings a pier directly in the center of the transept wall where it would be more natural to find a door. The five-part vault did not, therefore, become a general method of transept termination, though there is a very fine example of its survival in the church of Saint Urbain at Troyes (Aube) (cir. 1262-1300). It may even be that the desire for a regular elevation of the bays led to the subdivision of the transept by a row of central piers, such as those in the large church at Saint Nicolas-du-Port (Meurthe-et-Moselle) (sixteenth century)[6] and in a number of smaller examples, some of them of earlier date.[7]

SQUARE CHEVETS

Such a vault as that just described was, in a way, a sort of square chevet.[8] It was built to provide a better arrangement of windows in the terminal wall than would be possible beneath the transverse cell of a regular four- or six-part vault. Nor was its use confined to the transept for it is found with a varying number of cells at the end of the nave and choir as well. Such Norman churches as Saint Georges at Saint Martin-de-Boscherville (Fig. 51), Saint Étienne at Caen and Saint Cross at Winchester (choir cir. 1135-1189) are examples of this,[9] while the vaults of the transepts of Limburg Cathedral[10] (1235) and that of the chapter house at Boscherville (Fig. 52) resemble a chevet even more closely in that all but one of their severies are subdivided. When the ribs all rise from the same level, the appearance of such a vault is pleasing, but when,—as in the nave of Boscherville (Fig. 51),[11]—the intermediate ribs are shortened,

---

[6] Illustrated in Enlart, I, Fig. 318, opp. p. 588.

[7] Saint Jean-au-Bois (Oise) (twelfth century); Épinal (Vosges) (thirteenth century); Valentigny and Vendeuvre (Aube); Roberval, Vauciennes, and Verberie (Oise); Brunembert (Pas-de-Calais); etc.

[8] See p. 131, note 16 for explanation of the use of the word chevet.

[9] See also Tour (Calvados), Ch. Illustrated in Dehio and von Bezold, II, p. 187. Rys (Calvados), Ch. Baudot and Perrault-Dabot II, pl. 12; Omonville-la-Rogue, Ch. Baudot and Perrault-Dabot, II, pl. 46; Puiseaux (Loiret), Ch. Baudot and Perrault-Dabot, III, pl. 28.

[10] Hartung, III, pl. 134.

[11] There is a similar vault in the transept.

Fig. 51.—Saint Martin-de-Boscherville, Saint Georges.

Fig. 52.—Saint Martin-de-Boscherville, Saint Georges, Chapter-house.

the effect is very unsatisfactory, though this shortening of the ribs probably had a structural advantage in preventing the light from being partly
cut off, or the windows partly concealed by the radiants and the masonry
above them.

Vaulting of Semicircular Transepts

The vaulting of the transept naturally differs from that in the nave
when the former is given a semicircular termination.   In Romanesque
transepts of this type, the vaults are in the form either of simple half
domes, or of tunnel vaults ending in such domes, according as the transept
arms are lengthened or left merely in the form of apses.   Many churches
of both these types, but usually of small size, are to be found in southern
France,[12] while others appear in Italy and still others in the north of
Europe,[13] where such a church as that of Rolduc (Belgium) was considered by its builders as built in a Lombard manner, "scemate longo-
bardico,"[14] indicating that the semicircular transept was thought, at least,
to be of Lombard origin.   The most highly developed transepts of this
tunnel-vaulted, half-domed type are probably those in the church of Saint
Mary of the Capitol at Cologne, where a groin-vaulted ambulatory is
found around each transept apse.   Somewhat similar in plan are the
transepts of Tournai cathedral in Belgium (between cir. 1110-1170)
(Fig. 53), except that here the surrounding aisle is very narrow, and,
more important still, the half dome is replaced by a clumsy chevet vault
with very heavy ribs, their haunches raised to support a series of ramping
and contracting tunnel vaults.   This construction is very similar to the
framework of such a dome as that of the Baptistery at Florence.   Nor is
it without advantages, since it greatly reduces the vault thrusts and therefore renders unnecessary the use of flying-buttresses,[15] and at the same
time permits the windows to rise above the level of its impost.   The next
semicircular transept of importance is that of Noyon cathedral (cir.

[12] Among them: Lerins, Chapelle de la Trinité.   Illustrated in Revoil I, pl. 1; St. Martin-
de-Londres, Ch.   Revoil, I, pl. XXXIII.

[13] For example: Querqueville (Manche).

[14] See Lasteyrie, p. 530.

[15] An earlier transept with similar vaulting may have existed in church of St. Lucien
at Beauvais (1090-1109), but this church was unfortunately destroyed during the Revolution.   See Enlart, I, p. 480, note 3.

1140),[16] where there is a developed chevet of what will later be called the buttressing ribbed type.[17]   More developed still is the south transept of Soissons cathedral (1176-1207), which possesses an ambulatory in two stories with three bays of trapezoidal four-part ribbed vaults correspond-

FIG. 53.—TOURNAI, CATHEDRAL.

ing to each principal vaulting bay.   The transept proper is covered by a rectangular vault[18] and a broken-ribbed chevet with very broad window cells.   Other examples of semicircular transepts could be cited, both of the Romanesque and Gothic periods,[19] but either they do not present any vaulting forms not already discussed or they will be described in connection with the apse proper.   That the plan had a long lease of life, if not a very extensive usage, is shown by the fact that it appears in such seventeenth century churches as that of the Lycée Corneille at Rouen (beg. cir.

[16] Similar transepts at Breslau, Heiligekreuze; Paderborn, Cath.; Marburg, St. Elizabeth.
[17] The development and construction of chevet vaults is discussed in Chapter III.
[18] Apparently later than the chevet.
[19] See Enlart, I, p. 490 note 3 and Lasteyrie, pp. 285 and 522 for lists.   Also Neufchâtel (Seine Inférieure) fifteenth century.   Porter, II, p. 95.
[20] Plan in Gurlitt, p. 22.

1614),[20] and is found in numerous Renaissance churches in which the vaulting returns to the earlier tunnel and half-dome forms.[21]

THE VAULTS OF TRANSEPT AISLES AND CHAPELS

As the transept developed in importance aisles were added, sometimes merely along the east walls, but often along the west as well,[22] and even across the ends, especially in churches where such tribunes provided for a continuation of the triforium gallery.[23]   In such transepts the side aisles are vaulted just as those belonging to naves' of a corresponding period, and therefore require no discussion here.   More important are the chapels which open off of the transept, usually from the eastern wall. In general these consist of a semicircular apse either with or without one or more preceding bays.   During the Romanesque period such chapels were generally covered with a half dome sometimes preceded by a tunnel vault as in Saint Georges-de-Boscherville, while after the introduction of ribbed vaults, these and the chevet replace the tunnel vaults and half domes in their respective positions.   Sometimes the chapels are square, especially in Cistercian churches.   They are then covered either with tunnel vaults, as in Kirkstall Abbey, or with ribbed vaults in the Gothic period.   Usually all these radiating chapels are but one story in height, but in the cathedral of Laon, two beautiful chapels more than a semi-circle in plan and two stories in height appear, one at the east end of both the north and south aisles of the transept (Fig. 54).   These chapels are vaulted with seven-part chevets, and form, with the aisles and tribunes preceding them, veritable churches inside of the cathedral.   Chapels of similar character, but practically a full circle in plan and vaulted with a double chevet, are also to be seen in the two lower stories of the transept of Soissons cathedral.   They open off of the aisles and galleries through three slender arches, and the view into them from the transept proper affords one of the finest examples of Gothic perspective.

[21] See Enlart, I, p. 480 note 3 and Lasteyrie, pp. 285 and 522 for further examples.

[22] In rare instances, as in Saint Hilaire at Poitiers, there are aisles along the west wall only, but this is due to a rebuilding of the church.

[23] Toulouse, Saint Sernin; Reims, Saint Remi (originally) (see Lasteyrie, p. 282); Winchester, Cath. (1079-1093) (Rivoira, II, p. 205).   Tribunes are also to be seen in churches without a triforium gallery along the transept walls as for example in Saint Georges-de-Boscherville, Cerisy-la-Forêt (1030-1066), etc. See list in Enlart, I, p. 236, note 1.

CROSSING VAULTS

The intersection of the nave and transept was usually treated by the Romanesque builders as a distinctive vaulting bay. Occasionally, in the tunnel-vaulted churches, the builders allowed the vault of nave and transept to intersect and form a groined vault at the crossing, as, for example, in Saint Étienne at Beaugency (after 1050) (Loiret)[24] and in the church

FIG. 54.—LAON, CATHEDRAL, TRANSEPT TRIFORIUM CHAPEL.

of Boisney (Eure).[25] Groined vaults are also found in this position in certain churches, like those of the Rhenish provinces, where similar vaults are used in the nave. But as a general rule, the crossing of the Roman-

[24] See Lasteyrie, p. 539 and Enlart, I, p. 265, note 1.
[25] See Ruprich-Robert, II, p. 3.

esque church is covered by a dome resting on spherical pendentives or squinches, either unraised or else placed on a drum, which thus forms a lantern with windows to light the church interior.   There is no necessity for an extended discussion of raised and unraised domes, since as far as construction is concerned they differ only in the fact that when raised on a lantern they are somewhat more difficult to support because the vaults of choir, nave, and transept no longer serve as buttressing members.   The custom, however, of erecting a tower even above the raised domes offset to a large extent the thrusts which they created.

Sometimes these Romanesque crossing domes are of circular plan and supported on spherical pendentives.   These are common in the school of Perigord, where examples are afforded by the cathedral of Perigueux (Fig. 1) or the abbey church of Solignac.[26]   But the use of such domes on spherical pendentives was not confined to Perigord.   They are found in Poitou and Les Charentes, in the Southwest, and even in Limousin.[27] One of the best examples, and one in which there is a circular drum below the dome, appears in the church of Le Dorat (cir. middle twelfth century) (Haute-Vienne).[28]   Very occasionally, also, the flat triangular pendentive is used, as in Notre Dame at Chauvigny (Vienne).[29]

LANTERN TOWERS

The use of a lantern tower with windows opening into the church below its roof was destined to give rise to a number of interesting vaults. That such towers existed in France as early as the sixth century, is proved by the texts of Gregory of Tours and Fortunatus, in which such lanterns are mentioned as existing over the churches of Saint Martin at Tours, the cathedrals of Clermont-Ferrand, Narbonne, and Paris, as well as at Bordeaux and Nantes,[30] while Rivoira's contention[31] that the church of San Salvatore or del Crocifisso at Spoleto dates from the fourth century, if correct, would give an earlier though isolated Italian example of such a feature.   Whatever its origin, such a lantern was a particularly pleasing feature of church construction, especially in Romanesque churches,

[26] Lasteyrie, p. 271, Fig. 264.
[27] For other examples see Lasteyrie, p. 335, notes 3-4-5.
[28] Lasteyrie, p. 336, Fig. 359.
[29] See Lasteyrie, p. 270.
[30] See Enlart, I, pp. 123, 124.
[31] See Rivoira, II, pp. 27, 29.

which were without direct light in the nave and thus received a much needed addition to their interior illumination. It is not surprising, therefore, to find many of the more daring Romanesque builders including this central feature even in crossings with domes, as has already been noted. As a rule the pendentives were introduced beneath the wall of the clerestory drum which was therefore either of octagonal or circular plan. The examples of such lanterns are too numerous to cite though certain of them are worthy of some remark. In Auvergne, for example, in Notre Dame-du-Port at Clermont-Ferrand (Figs. 49, 50), at Orcival (Puy-de-Dôme),[32] Saint Nectaire (Puy-de-Dôme),[33] and elsewhere the system of transept and crossing vaulting already described[34] made possible the introduction of windows in either the east or west walls of the central towers, or both, though rarely in those to the north or the south, where there were half or full tunnel vaults to abut the dome. In two churches of Central France, those at Benevent-l'Abbaye (Creuse)[35] and Le Dorat (Haute Vienne),[36] the lanterns are especially beautiful. They are covered with domes raised on a drum supported upon spherical pendentives. In such churches, where there is no direct light in the nave, the lantern adds much to the appearance of an otherwise oppressively dark interior.

RIBBED DOMES

Another lantern of interest is to be seen in southern France in the cathedral of Notre Dame-des-Doms at Avignon (probably cir. middle of twelfth century).[37] Here the transepts are narrower than the nave and in order to make the crossing square, a series of four arches has been thrown across between the spandrels of the nave and choir arches, Over the square thus formed is an octagonal lantern on squinches which in turn supports a circular dome with the unusual feature of a series of flat pilaster-like ribs along its under surface. Such ribs are, of course, largely decorative and correspond to those found in the apses of many neighboring churches.[38] True ribbed domes were also used as a means

[32] Lasteyrie, p. 445, Fig. 463.
[33] Lasteyrie, p, 316, Fig. 338.
[34] See p. 106.
[35] Lasteyrie, p. 249, Fig. 239.
[36] Lasteyrie, p. 336, Fig. 359.
[37] See also Marseilles,—La Major.
[38] See p. 124.

of covering the crossing,[39] and this is but natural in view of the fact that such domes were quite frequently employed over circular churches,

FIG. 55.—LAON, CHURCH OF THE TEMPLARS.

as for example Saint Sepulchre at Cambridge, and the Templar's Chapel at Laon (Fig. 55),[40] while half domes of similar character appear over many apses of the Transitional period.[41]

LOBED DOMES

Similar domes to that just described at Avignon are quite common in Spain, where for that matter the lantern itself had a very remarkable development. Thus in the cathedral of Zamora (consecrated 1144) there is a dome with sixteen ribs. It is not of perfectly simple type, however, for the masonry between the ribs is curved slightly outward, giving it the

[39] Either with or without a lantern beneath them. Examples: Montagne (Gironde); Nantille, Notre Dame; Saumur, St. Pierre. See Michel, II, p. 108 and Lasteyrie, p. 479.

[40] See also such other buildings as the Château de Simiane (Basses-Alpes) (apparently twelfth century). Illustrated in Revoil, III, pl. VIII.

[41] See p. 125.

form of a lobed dome.[42] The lobes are comparatively small, but otherwise not unlike such larger ones as those in SS. Sergius and Bacchus at Constantinople (cir. 527) and the Serapeum of the Villa Adriana at Tivoli (125-135). As far as construction is concerned this arrangement made it possible to lay up the masonry between the ribs with little or no centering, so that once the ribs were in place, the task of completing the dome was a comparatively simple one. Unlike the "Gothic dome" which is later discussed, the thrusts were not materially decreased by the lobed plan and in its essentials the dome thus formed was precisely like the simple type. From the point of view of appearance these Spanish lanterns are certainly very beautiful. Usually pierced with windows in twelve out of the sixteen bays, and sometimes, as at Salamanca, with a few windows in the lower of the two stages forming the drum, they admit a great quantity of light to the very heart of the church where its presence is most needed. Moreover, the spherical pendentives from which the lanterns rise are more pleasing than the squinches generally found in France.

"Gothic Domes" or Double Chevets

Because of its resemblance to such ribbed domes as those just described it may be well to discuss here what may be called a "Gothic dome" if such a term be permissible. This is, in other words, the familiar chevet vault extended to cover a space of circular or octagonal plan. One of these vaults of circular plan and with eight ribs appears over the crossing of Saint Nicolas at Blois (Fig. 56). Unlike the ribbed dome, its masonry courses are not horizontal and concentric with the impost line, but practically at right angles to it, thus giving wall arches whose crowns are nearly as high as the central keystone itself. Each window cell is thus precisely like one-quarter of a four-part cross-ribbed vault. It was this form of double chevet vault which was frequently used as late as the Renaissance period in Italy, where it appears in such works as the Pazzi chapel at Florence (cir. 1420) (Fig. 57) and elsewhere though without

---

[42] Similar domes may be seen in the old cathedral of Salamanca (finished before 1178). (Moore, Character of Renaissance Architecture, p. 57, Fig. 28.) [Street, (Fig. 7, op. p. 80) shows this dome as having flat severies, and does not mention the fact that they are curved, as he takes pains to do in regard to Zamora] ; and the collegiate church at Toro (begun cir. 1160-1170, finished in thirteenth century), (Michel, II, p. 108, Fig. 76). It is difficult to tell from the photograph whether this last example has the lobed vault surface.

FIG. 56.—BLOIS, SAINT NICHOLAS.

FIG. 57.—FLORENCE, PAZZI CHAPEL.

any wall rib. These "Gothic domes" were frequently polygonal as well as circular. Thus in the cathedral of Worms (Fig. 58) there is an octagonal lantern, on squinches, surmounted by a vault with eight cells of decidedly domical type, the whole being only slightly different from a

FIG. 58.—WORMS, CATHEDRAL.

lobed dome. A more developed double chevet, dating from the second half of the fifteenth century, appears over the crossing of the cathedral of Evreux (Eure),[43] where there is also a complete system of ribs.[44] The form of the pendentives is that of flat triangles, and they are decorated with elaborate designs in flamboyant tracery. Similar flat triangles but with a series of mouldings at the top, are used to support the octagonal lantern of Coutances cathedral (Fig. 59), perhaps the most beautiful in France, and apparently dating from the second half of the thirteenth century. Its vault is in sixteen cells, two to each lantern wall, and each

[43] Illustrated in Simpson, II, p. 104.
[44] There is an earlier and somewhat similar crossing vault in the church of S. Marien at Gelnhausen (1225-on) Hartung, III, pl. 145.

containing a lofty window, the whole clerestory rising above a lower stage of coupled arches with a narrow passage behind them.

A crossing vault of similar character, but with a change in the arrangement of the ribs, which form an eight-pointed star around a central

Fig. 59.—Coutances, Cathedral.

octagonal opening, is to be seen in the cathedral of Saragossa in Spain (after 1500),[45] while the final stage in such vaulting, in which the ribs become merely a framework beneath a flat ceiling, but nevertheless a framework of elaborate and beautiful design, may be seen over the crossing of the cathedral of Burgos (finished 1568).[46]

Square Lanterns with Eight-Part Vaults

There now remain for discussion lantern towers of square plan. This was the form almost universally employed in Normandy, England, and churches which came under Norman influence, especially in the earlier Gothic period. During the Romanesque epoch such lanterns were wooden roofed. But with the introduction of the ribbed vault, an eight-part vault was devised for this crossing, whose severies were precisely like those

---

[45] Michel, IV, p. 829, Fig. 546.
[46] Michel, IV, p. 828, Fig. 545.

above the windows in six-part vaulting, from which, in fact, this new type probably developed.

Most of the towers originally wooden roofed have since been vaulted, and it is therefore difficult to judge of their original character. Their imposing interior appearance, however, may be judged from the ruins of the abbey church of Jumièges (1040-1067). It would seem, from the places, for beam ends left in the wall, that such lanterns as this were generally roofed with a flat ceiling above the first stage of openings, the second series probably forming a belfry. It is natural, therefore, when vaulting comes in, to find it placed at the level of the former flat ceiling with only the lower openings used as windows, leaving the walls above to offset the thrusts of the vault by their downward pressure. A somewhat rudimentary vault of this eight-part character may be seen in Saint Georges-de-Boscherville,[47] in which the wall arches are omitted and all the ribs made to spring from corbels. This, of course, is because the Norman Romanesque crossings were not originally planned for vaulting. A little later, wall ribs were regularly used, and in Saint Yved at Braisne (consecrated 1215)[48] the four major ribs have their supports running all the way to the floor, while in the cathedral of Laon (after 1165) (Fig. 60) even the eight wall ribs which rise from the corners of the tower are similarly carried down. Of course the intermediate ribs necessarily rise from corbels, but in the developed crossings of this type such corbels are placed as near as possible to the crowns of the four great arches of the nave, choir, and transepts. Similar lanterns are to be seen in the church of Notre Dame at Cluny, and in Saint Maclou at Rouen (lantern cir. 1511),[49] where, however, ridge ribs are added in each of the eight cells.

Notwithstanding the examples cited, the use of a lantern is not common in developed Gothic architecture. This is perhaps due to the fact that the rapidly increasing size of the clerestory made such an addition to the lighting equipment unnecessary, though it is more probable that the great height of many of the churches rendered the construction of a tower over the crossing a dangerous undertaking. Even in the less lofty churches of

[47] It is possible that this vault is of wood.
[48] Simpson, II, Fig. 68, opp. p. 104.
[49] Simpson, II, Fig. 69, opp. p. 164.

England, where a central tower is almost invariably found, the latter is frequently closed from below by a vault.

RIB-VAULTED CROSSINGS WITH NO LANTERNS

Where there is no lantern, the vault of the crossing is generally a continuation of that of the nave or transepts. It is, therefore, often of simple four-part cross-ribbed type, with or without a domed up crown.[50]

FIG. 60.—LAON, CATHEDRAL.

Certain of the Gothic builders, however, even in the early thirteenth century, realized the advantage to be gained by subdividing the cells of the crossing vault with ridge ribs. Hence in the abbey church of Fossanova (consecrated in 1208),[51] as well as in those at Casamari and Arbona[52] in

---

[50] Examples are furnished by: Florence, S. M. Novella; Sens, Cath. (Fig. 28); Paris, N. D.; Soissons, Cath.; Cologne, Cath.; to cite but a few churches.

[51] Cummings, II, p. 141, Fig. 330.

[52] Cummings, II, p. 149, Fig. 335.

Italy, and in many churches of France,[53] especially those of Anjou type,[54] transverse and longitudinal ridge ribs were used and in most instances the vault was considerably domed up. In Amiens cathedral (cir. 1265) the crossing vault, nearly forty feet square and about one hundred and forty feet from the ground, was further subdivided by a single pair of tiercerons in each of the major severies, and the eight central panels thus formed were raised at the crown to reduce the thrusts of the vault as well as the amount of centering necessary for its construction. After its introduction at Amiens this form of crossing was quite extensively employed, sometimes with its ridge ribs running completely across the bay, as for example, in Auxerre cathedral, sometimes running only to the keystone of the tiercerons, as in Bayonne and Troyes cathedrals or Saint Euverte at Orleans.

With the use of many added ribs in other portions of the church, came a corresponding elaboration in the vaults of the crossing. Thus many examples might be cited of lierne and tierceron vaulting in all degrees of complexity, especially in England,[55] while fan vaulting is to be seen in the abbey church of Bath (cir. 1500-1590),[56] and pendant vaults of elaborate character in Saint Étienne-du-Mont at Paris (probably cir. 1550-1600). Occasionally also the transept is subdivided by a central row of piers in which case the vault of the crossing is in two bays.[57] It is unnecessary, however, to discuss at length these exceptional crossing types since they do not differ structurally from the vaulting systems already described in connection with the nave.

[53] For example in Dol, Cath.; Etampes, Saint Gilles; Bayeux, Cath., etc.

[54] For example in Angers, Cath. (Fig. 19) : Bordeaux, Saint Michel, etc.

[55] Numerous illustrations may be found in Bond, Gothic Architecture in England and English Church Architecture.

[56] Most of the vaulting is modern but built as originally planned.

[57] An example of this arrangement may be seen at Saint Nicolas-du-Port (Meurthe-et-Moselle). Enlart, Fig. 318, opp. p. 588.

CHAPTER III

APSE VAULTS

The traditional method of terminating the church edifice at the end reserved for the clergy was by means of a semicircular or polygonal apse, and this method, which was of Roman origin, continued to be followed in the majority of Romanesque and Gothic churches. Such apses gave to the interior of the edifice a more dignified appearance than was possible with a flat east wall, by avoiding the abrupt termination which the latter produced and by emphasizing the central point in the sanctuary, which was occupied by the high altar in most of the mediaeval churches.

Apses Vaulted with Half Domes

Once adopted from Roman architecture as a standard part of the church plan, the construction of the apse was naturally based upon Roman models, and since these were always vaulted with a half dome of masonry, similar half domes were employed by the Christian builders of the early mediaeval period. During the Romanesque era, these half domes were almost always of stone laid in horizontal courses, supported by substantial walls of semicircular or polygonal plan. They opened directly into a transept or a tunnel-vaulted choir. The earliest of these half domes were of semicircular elevation, but the pointed form made its appearance in the late eleventh or early twelfth century in many churches. In both forms, the principles of construction are the same.

Lighting Problems Connected with the Construction of Half Domed Apses

It is a characteristic of the half dome that it exerts a large amount of downward pressure and but little outward thrust, particularly if it be of pointed section. For this reason, such a vault requires a firm support but only a slight amount of buttressing. As long, therefore, as the half dome rested directly upon comparatively low exterior walls, it had plenty of support, and it was even possible to pierce the walls with windows without endangering its stability. But with the increase in height of the more developed Romanesque churches and the introduction of ambulatories, it became difficult to light the sanctuary and still retain the half dome.

Two methods were evolved for overcoming this difficulty. The first, which may be seen in the abbey church at Cunault (Maine-et-Loire) (second half of twelfth century),[1] consisted in the construction of a lofty ambulatory opening into the apse through arches rising to the impost of the half dome, or even slightly above it, and resting upon piers of as slender proportions as possible, so that, although the sanctuary was deprived of all direct light, a certain amount was obtained from windows in the outer wall of the ambulatory or from the radiating chapels, while, at the same time, the vault of this ambulatory aided in the support of the apse and vice versa. Such a system, though structurally correct, was not entirely satisfactory. The sanctuary and choir were the portions of the church most in need of lighting, since they contained the altar and the seats for the monks or clergy by whom the services were chanted, and indirect light was bound to be insufficient.

The second method, which may be seen in the church of Saint Savin (Vienne) (eleventh century),[2] consisted in reducing the height of the ambulatory, even when this involved making it lower than the side aisles, and then placing a clerestory above the ambulatory arches beneath the springing of the half dome. This may be considered as the best type of apsidal termination developed during the purely Romanesque period. It was only when the half dome was discarded that a satisfactory solution was finally reached in the development of the chevet vault. There were, however, two important series of ribbed half domes, the second of which, at least, may have had some bearing upon the evolution of the chevet type.

Apses with Ribbed Half Domes

The first series lies largely in southern France in the Romanesque school of Provence. Here there are a certain number of churches, among them the chapel of Saint Honorat in Les Alyscamps at Arles (Bouches-

---

[1] See also Poitiers, Saint Hilaire (Fig. 7) and Notre Dame-la-Grande, etc.

[2] See also Toulouse, Saint Sernin; Saint Benoit--sur-Loire (Fig. 13) ; and Nevers, St. Étienne, etc.

du-Rhone) (eleventh century?), in which the surface of the half dome is broken out at regular intervals into a number of flat, pilaster-like, radiating strips, forming a part of the actual masonry of the vault. These divide the half dome in much the same manner as true Gothic ribs, but they do not support it in any way and seem to have been used for the decoration which such a change in the surface of the vault produced.[3] As a general rule, these ribs radiate from a point slightly back from the crown of the apse arch and often from a raised masonry ring as in the chapel just cited. They vary, however, both in number, thickness and width, some being comparatively thick and widening out from the central keystone as in the cathedral of Notre Dame-des-Doms at Avignon (Vaucluse), others being but slightly salient and of the same width throughout like those in Saint Honorat at Arles.

Much larger in number and extent is the second series of churches with rib-vaulted apses, though they are in general of later date than those in Provence. Their radiants have a certain structural character, for they are independent of the vault surface and were doubtless erected in most cases as a permanent centering to aid in the construction of the half dome. They do not, however, aid to any extent in its support, for the courses of masonry in the vaults are still horizontal and concentric with the curve of the apse, and the completed half domes would therefore stand just as well were the ribs removed. It may be that they were introduced in order to make the apse correspond more closely in appearance with the ribbed vault which had in many cases been introduced in the naves of the churches in which the ribbed half domes are found. In any event, they mark a stage in apse vaulting between the simple half dome and the developed chevet, which is worthy of careful consideration. Most of these vaults date from the second quarter of the twelfth century and are to be found within the zone of influence of the Ile-de-France, though occasionally an example is found at a long distance from this center as in the case of Sant' Abondio

---

[3] They may have been inspired by the salient arches of such a tunnel vault as that in the Temple of Diana at Nimes, and in any event would seem to owe their origin to classic prototypes and to be largely decorative, a theory which is strengthened by the appearance of such a vault as that in the little church of Saint Jean-de-Moustier, at Arles (probably of the ninth cenury) (Revoil, I, pl. XVI), where these radiants very closely resemble Corinthian pilasters.

at Como,[4] Santa Maria di Castello at Corneto-Tarquinia in Italy,[5] and such churches as that of the Monasterio de la Oliva (Navarra) in Spain,[6] (1198). The number of ribs varies considerably, though two is most common particularly in the smaller churches and chapels.[7] Of these, the church at Morienval (Oise) (Fig. 77) furnishes a good, though recently reconstructed, example, while Saint Georges-de-Boscherville (Fig. 61) may be cited as possessing a large apse of similar character.

The important thing in a comparison of these two vaults is the difference in the lighting of the completed apse. At Boscherville, it was a simple matter to pierce the exterior wall with windows, in this case in two stages, and still keep their crowns practically below the level of the impost of the half dome, since the latter rested directly upon the outer walls. But at Morienval there was an ambulatory, and in order to get a clerestory above its arches, the windows had to be cut into the curved surface of the half dome itself, with the result that they were so deep as to prove of only limited usefulness. Other examples could be cited where this same attempt is made to obtain sufficiently large windows by shoving their heads into the half dome,[8] while at Beaulieu (Corrèze)[9] the windows lie entirely above the impost.

Besides the ribbed half dome just described, there is still another type to be seen in the Lady chapel of the church of Saint Martin-des-Champs at Paris (Fig. 65). Its plan is a trefoil and the vault is made up of a series

[4] Dartein, pl. 76.

[5] Porter, Cons. of Lombard and Gothic Vaults, Fig. 62. There are also a number of churches of the more developed period in which somewhat similar ribbed half domes are found, though these are frequently laid up in flat gores over polygonal apses. Examples include: Worms, Cath.; west apse, see Fig. 58; Florence, Cath. east and transept apses.

[6] Madrazo-Gurlitt, pl. 178.

[7] Examples include Berzy-le-Sec and Laffaux (Aisne); Chelles (Oise) and Bonnes (Vienne) all dating cir. 1140-1150; Bruyères, and Vauxrezis (Aisne) probably of about the same date, and Torcy (Aisne) dating from the second half of the twelfth century; Étampes, St. Martin, radiating chapel. All of these are illustrated in Lefevre-Pontalis. Examples with three ribs include Thor (Vaucluse) and Saint Pierre-de-Reddes (Hérault), both illustrated in Revoil. Example with four ribs, Como, Sant' Abondio. Example with five ribs, Montmajour (Bouches-du-Rhône), Ab. Ch. Revoil, II, pl. XXXI. For further examples, see Porter, II, p. 78.

[8] For instance, at Vieil-Arcy, Ch. (Lefevre-Pontalis, pl. XLV), where there are no ribs beneath the half dome; and in the last five churches with two ribs listed in the preceding note.

[9] Lasteyrie, p. 450, Fig. 470.

of segments of domes with salient ribs marking their intersections. As far as construction is concerned, there is really no change from that of the more common half dome, for the courses of masonry are still horizontal and the ribs merely serve as centering and as a means of subdividing the

FIG. 61.—SAINT MARTIN-DE-BOSCHERVILLE, SAINT GEORGES.

surface to be vaulted and clearly marking the lines of intersection. The vault would stand equally well were the ribs removed and is, in structural character, very similar to the celled domes of the Villa Adriana at Tivoli and of S.S. Sergius and Bacchus at Constantinople.

"GROINED HALF DOMES"

Another form of apse vault of which there would seem to be a number of examples prior to the introduction of ribbed vaulting may perhaps be termed the "groined half dome." It is a vault resembling a segmental dome except that the segments do not run down to a common impost, but form a series of window cells not unlike those of a groined vault but not running all the way to the vault crown. The earliest of these vaults appears to be that in the crypt of Saint Laurent at Grenoble (Isère) (sixth century).[10] Rivoira has shown[11] that Roman prototypes of this form can be found in the so-called "Temple di Siepe" (second century) at Rome, the vestibule of the Villa Adriana at Tivoli (125-135) and elsewhere. There are also a number of Romanesque examples. Of these, one is in the chapel off the south transept of Saint Nicholas at Caen (1080-1093),[12] while another is to be found in Saint Andrew's chapel at Canterbury cathedral (cir. 1110).[13] These vaults closely resemble the true Gothic chevet which was soon to follow them, and they might seem to be its prototypes were it not for the fact that their construction is of an entirely different character. All are built of small stone or rubble and were undoubtedly laid up on a wooden centering with no particular regard for the direction in which the masonry courses ran, or possibly with these courses like those in a half dome. The construction was thus a combination of half dome and groined vaulting and not at all of the ribbed type. That they may, however, have been of influence in the development of the true chevet will be later suggested.

Apses with Four-Part Ribbed Vaults

A final type of rather primitive vaulting which was subsequent to the introduction of ribbed vaulting but would seem to be prior to the use or at least to the extensive knowledge of the chevet, consisted in the employment of a simple four-part vault over the semicircle of the apse (Plate II-a).[14] The result was an awkward kind of chevet vault which is worthy of consideration as perhaps having a part in the development of the true Gothic form. It might properly be called a four-part cross-ribbed apse vault.

[10] Rivoira, II, p. 38, Fig. 399.

[11] Rivoira, II, pp. 39-40.

[12] Rivoira, II, p. 93.

[13] Moore, Mediaeval Church Architecture of England, p. 15, Fig. 11.

[14] Forest-l' Abbaye (Somme) (plan in Enlart, I, p. 447, Fig. 211) furnishes one example of this and others are listed in Enlart, I, p. 447 and note 2 at the foot of that page.

PLATE II

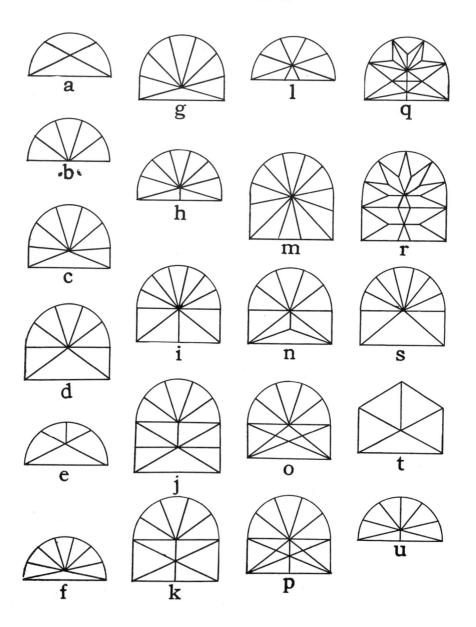

The Chevet Vault

By the middle of the twelfth century, all the methods of apse vaulting thus far described, were abandoned[15] in favor of the ribbed Gothic chevet[16] which was then developed. In this new vault the masonry courses are no longer horizontal and concentric but run in a generally perpendicular direction from a series of radiating ribs, which have a common keystone, to a wall rib or a curved line of intersection above the heads of a series of apse windows in whole or in part above the level of the impost of the radiants. In other words, the chevet vault consists of a series of triangular severies, each essentially like one quarter of a four-part cross-ribbed vault.

The evolution of this developed chevet from the earlier types of apse vaulting already discussed is difficult to trace and in fact it seems most reasonable to imagine that it was a spontaneous transformation which did not require any intermediate steps. It has, for instance, been pointed out that the greatest problem of the apse builder was to place a clerestory of good sized windows above the ambulatory arcade or at least as high as possible in the apse wall and at the same time to keep the pressures and thrusts of his vault at the lowest possible point. Imagine then a builder with this in mind starting to construct a ribbed half dome with windows rising above its impost. Suppose that the radiating ribs were first constructed and the space to be vaulted thus divided into triangular compartments. Now assume that the builder was familiar with the four-part cross-ribbed vault—a reasonable assumption since everything seems to point to an earlier date for such vaults than for the ribbed chevet. Would he not be prompt to see that a series of clerestory windows could be built around the apse precisely like those along the walls of nave or choir and each triangular space thus formed, be covered by one quarter of four-part vault? Is not this especially reasonable in view of the fact that there existed groined vaults of just this type,[17] exactly as there existed groined prototypes out of which sprang the simple four-part cross-ribbed vault?

[15] There are occasionally to be found some late examples showing the survival of the half dome as an apse vault, but these are exceptional after cir. 1150, until the Renaissance period.

[16] The word chevet is used here and elsewhere as referring to the ribbed vaulting developed and applied to the apse of the Gothic churches.

[17] See p. 128, 129.

Furthermore, if the peculiar four-part apse vaults described as sometimes employed in transitional churches are any or all of them earlier than the earliest of the true chevets, would it not seem as if the builders were bent upon using quadripartite vaulting of some form, even over the apse, in order to obtain a clerestory? Whatever the true process of evolution may have been, it is at least possible that the above explanations are correct and that the chevet vault developed directly from the difficulty of placing windows beneath the ribbed half dome. If such was the case another type of vault would seem to have owed its origin in large part to the lighting problem.

Types of Chevet Vaults

Once introduced, four types of chevet vault were gradually established, not counting the variation which each of them underwent. For convenience, these will be called the radiating-ribbed type, the broken-ribbed type, the buttressing-ribbed type, and finally the diagonal or cross-ribbed type. Each will be considered in turn and an effort made to trace their consecutive development.

The chronology of these vaults is very difficult to determine. In fact, it is probably safe to assume that the earliest example, if there were not a number of these vaults simultaneously constructed, has disappeared. In any event, it would seem that the vault must have been first used somewhere between 1130 and 1150 as there are several existing examples which date from this period. If these cannot be arranged in any certain order, they may at least, be used to show the form of the early chevets.

Radiating-Ribbed Chevets

Perhaps the most primitive, in appearance at least, is that above the transept of Tournai cathedral (Fig. 53) in which, as has been noted,[18] the extrados of each rib is built up until it forms a flat sloping upper surface, each cell of the vault proper rising from the ramps thus formed. Next to this vault at Tournai, and as a matter of fact, probably of earlier date though of more developed type are the two chevet vaults of Largny (Aisne) (cir. 1140).[19] and Azy-Bonneil (Aisne),[20]—which are three-

---

[18] See p. 110.
[19] Lefevre-Pontalis, pl. XXIX.
[20] Lefevre-Pontalis, pl. LI.

celled,—and the one in the lower story of the chapel of the Bishop's palace at Laon (cir. 1137-1147) (Fig. 62) with five cells. The latter shows their general characteristics. There are no wall ribs and the round-headed windows are only partly raised above the impost of the radiants while there

FIG. 62.—LAON, CHAPEL OF THE BISHOP'S PALACE.

abut against the keystone of the apsidal arch (Plate II-b). It will be noticed also that this arch is greatly thickened to resist the pressure of these ribs, and at Tournai is preceded by a tunnel-vaulted bay to make this resistance even more secure.[21]

But much more important than these smaller chevet vaults, are those of a number of large churches, also belonging to the second quarter of the twelfth century. Of these, Saint Germer-de-Fly[22] (Fig. 63) has been most prominently brought to notice through Mr. Moore's work on Gothic architecture. It is doubly of interest because it possesses chevet vaults of two distinct stages in the development of this new form. Thus in the original radiating chapels opening off the ambulatory,[23] three-part chevet

[21] At Laon the remaining bays of the chapel are groined and if their vaults are original, this presents one of the few examples of a church completely groined and especially of one with the combination of groined vault and ribbed chevet.

[22] Moore, Mediaeval Church Architecture of England, pl. 1, opp. p. 19. Variously dated 1130-1150.

[23] Illustrated in Moore, pp. 72 and 73, Figs. 26, 27.

vaults of the type described in the previous paragraph were employed, with
this advance, namely the introduction of stilted, round-headed wall ribs.
The vaults are still highly domed at the crown and it would seem very
reasonable to suppose that they were completed before the vault of the
great apse was begun.

This latter shows an advance in construction beyond that hitherto seen.

FIG. 63.—SAINT GERMER-DE-FLY, ABBEY CHURCH.

In the first place, the entire window is placed above the level of the impost
of the radiants with a consequent raising of the vault surface above the
windows and a great reduction in its domed-up character. The line of
intersection of the vault cell with the apse wall, which is marked by a
slightly pointed, stilted wall rib, resting upon slender shafts rising from the
clerestory string-course, is almost perpendicular from the impost of the
radiants to a point about at their haunch. Thus the lower portion of the
masonry panel is really a flat wall resting upon the ribs. The object of the

builders in thus constructing their vault panels would seem to have been twofold, first to get a large space of pleasing shape for clerestory windows and secondly to aid in overcoming the thrusts of the radiating ribs. The first is perhaps the less important of the two, for the windows in the early chevets very rarely occupy all the space beneath the wall intersection. The second, however, furnishes a much better explanation of this form of panel.   And this explanation would seem to lie, not so much in the fact that the stilted wall rib concentrated the thrust along a narrow strip of exterior wall where it could be met by exterior buttresses[24] but rather in the fact that the weight of such a flat wall, rising perpendicularly above the radiating ribs, practically offset all of their outward thrusts by its downward pressure while the little which remained was taken care of by the thick walls characteristic of church construction in the Transitional period.   Thus it is possible to account for the almost total lack of exterior abutment in such apses as this at Saint Germer-de-Fly, where only the slenderest of shafts are found along the exterior wall serving far more for decoration than for abutment.[25]   That the stilting was not done primarily to concentrate the thrusts is further shown by the fact that in many of the later Gothic churches which were built long after the flying-buttress was perfected there is no attempt to stilt the wall rib, but the masonry of the vault is actually curved outward from the very springing of the radiants, which are raised to the impost of the window heads to give the vault this form.[26]

The highly stilted wall intersection with the consequent elevation of the clerestory window and flattening of the lower part of the vault cell constitutes the great structural advance in the chevet of Saint Germer.   The employment of the wall rib, however, introduces an important matter for discussion.   To be sure this is not by any means the first example of its use, for formerets may be found even in groined vaults, but it is one of the early examples on a large scale and may serve to introduce the question as to the part which these ribs played in Gothic architecture.

[24] See Moore, p. 130, et seq., and Porter, II, p. 80.

[25] See also the apses of Saint Étienne at Caen, of Saint Martin-des-Champs at Paris and of Soissons cathedral transept. Other churches were probably originally designed without the flying-buttresses, among them Saint Remi at Reims.   See Porter, II, p. 209 (from Lefevre-Pontalis).

[26] This type of vault is later discussed. See p. 153.

The Use of Wall Ribs in Gothic Ribbed Vaulting

It has generally been maintained that the wall ribs were integral and important members of a true ribbed vault and that they actually aided in the support of the masonry panels. There are, however, a number of reasons for believing that this is not entirely so but that these ribs were comparatively unimportant as far as their relation to the vaults was concerned and were of much more importance, in the first place as cover joints, in the second as window heads, and in the third as relieving arches in the clerestory wall. Two important facts lend strength to the theory that the wall rib was not as a rule a supporting member. The first of these lies in the fact that it was quite frequently omitted even from vaults of the true Gothic form, and the second, in the fact that, when present, there are perhaps as many cases in which the curve of the vault fails to follow that of the rib as there are of the reverse condition. In fact, it is a question whether in the majority of cases the vault panel actually rests upon or even cuts into the face of the formeret. Take, for example, a number of chevet vaults[27] and examine them in this respect. At Saint Germer (Fig. 63) the wall rib is largely a relieving arch in the clerestory wall which is made much thinner beneath it; and while the curve of the chevet cells follows in general that of the arch, it does not exactly correspond with it. In the large chevet vault of Saint Remi at Reims (Fig. 64), and in many other vaults not over the apse, especially in the English churches and those in which a group of clerestory windows is found in each bay, no wall rib is used, showing that such a rib was not at all necessary as far as the construction and support of the vault was concerned. Moreover, in many of the churches in which a wall rib is used along the exact line of the vault surface, it is too small to act as a supporting member and would seem to be merely a cover-joint to hide the intersection of the vault surface with the clerestory wall.[28] Finally and most important of all are the cases in which this rib is used primarily as a window head. In some of these, as

---

[27] The chevet vault is chosen for this discussion merely because the photographs are handy for reference. Similar vaults coult, however, be found in all the other portions of the church.

[28] For example, in Soissons transept. It certain other examples, the formeret does not follow the vault curve. See Paris, St. Martin-des-Champs (Fig. 65), Noyon transept, etc.

for example in the apse of La Madeleine at Vézelay, and those of the cathedrals of Soissons (Fig. 67) and Chartres (Fig. 68), the curve of the vault corresponds with this window-head arch, but in many other apses such as those of Bourges cathedral (Fig. 76), of Saint Étienne at Caen (Fig. 70), and of the Sainte Chapelle at Saint Germer, the builders without hesitation curved their vault surface away from the line of the window-

FIG. 64.—REIMS, SAINT REMI.

head which would otherwise be the natural wall rib.[29] Although from the preceding facts, it would seem evident that the wall rib was not an essential structural member of the Gothic vaulting system it may have been of advantage in many instances for holding a temporary wooden centering during the construction of the vault panels.

RADIATING-RIBBED CHEVETS CONTINUED

Returning again to the radiating-ribbed chevet, especially that of Saint Germer-de-Fly (Fig. 63), it is important to note the one great weakness which this vault possesses. It lies in the position of the radiating ribs which abut the apsidal arch at its crown, in other words at a point not at all

[29] A vault of similar character may be noted in the name of Amiens and numerous other instances could be cited outside of the chevet vaults.

suited to meet the pressures which are thus brought to bear against it. A rather heavy arch between the apse and the remaining bay of the choir, though no heavier than those in the vaulted bays of the nave, aids in resisting the pressure but nevertheless such a vault is not strictly logical from a structural standpoint. It is not as well buttressed, for example, as the ribbed half dome of Saint Georges at Boscherville (Fig. 61), or the transept chevet at Tournai (Fig. 53), in which a tunnel vaulted bay precedes the arch against whose crown the radiants are brought to bear.

It is not surprising that this vault was but little used in subsequent Gothic architecture. It is possible, however, to cite a few examples, among them the cathedrals of Séez (Orne) (end of the thirteenth century), Cambrai (Nord) (cir. 1250), and Dinan (Cotes-du-Nord) (end of the thirteenth century), the cathedral of Saint Sauveur at Bruges (Belgium) (probably thirteenth century), and the abbey church of Moissac (Tarn) (probably fourteenth century). There is also a peculiar form in which the ribs are narrowed toward the crown, in Santa Maria sopra Minerva at Rome (after 1285). Two other slight variants of the type, one in the church of Saint Pierre-le-Guillard at Bourges and the other in the cathedral of Moulins are later discussed.

Broken-Ribbed Chevets

After that of Saint Germer-de-Fly, perhaps the next important chevet is that of Saint Martin-des-Champs at Paris (Fig. 65), which dates from about 1140-1150 and may possibly be the earliest of what will be termed broken-ribbed chevets. On the exterior, this apse closely resembles Saint Germer with no flying-buttresses and only very light exterior buttress-shafts. In the interior, however, there is a marked difference between the two, for the apse of Saint Martin-des-Champs is so constructed as to include not merely the bays actually on the curve, but one rectangular bay of the choir as well. The builders thus set themselves the problem of constructing a chevet vault with seven cells, over a space greater than a semicircle. If they had made all the radiants of such a vault meet at the crown of the transverse arch, there would have been a great disparity in the length of the ribs and a very awkward shape to the separate vault cells. To avoid this, and to do away with the pressure of the radiants at the crown of the apsidal arch, the builders moved the keystone of the radiating ribs back from this crown to a point where all of them become nearly equal in length. And since the bay with parallel sides was of practically the same size as four[30] of those making up the apse proper, the keystone fell very nearly on the transverse line between the two piers marking the eastern end

FIG. 65.—PARIS, SAINT MARTIN-DES-CHAMPS.

of this bay (Plate II-c). In none of the chevets of this type did it fall directly at the center of such a line, however, and it is this fact that differentiates the chevet vaults of broken-ribbed character from the slightly later and more developed buttressing-ribbed type. A vault like that at Saint Martin-des-Champs, marks an advance over that at Saint Germer in that the two western ribs furnish admirable abutment for the keystone of the vault, and the added choir bay gives a more spacious appearance to this portion of the church.

There is another example of this broken-ribbed chevet in Paris, in the church of Saint Germain-des-Pres (cir. 1163), while still others may be

[30] The eastern bay in this particular church was widened to give a broad opening into the Lady chapel.

seen in Saint Quiriace at Provins (cir. 1160) (Fig. 31) and in La Madeleine at Vézelay (cir. 1140-1180) (Fig. 66). The latter is of especial
interest because it shows some peculiar makeshifts in the matter of construction. Here the choir would seem to have been originally designed to

FIG. 66.—VÉZELAY, LA MADELEINE.

consist of two rectangular bays with four-part vaults and an apse of five
sides probably with a chevet like that at Saint Germer.[31]   But by the time
the western bay of the choir had been built up to the clerestory, it would
seem as if a new idea of a seven-part chevet had come in, perhaps from
Paris, and the next bay was subdivided so as to give seven equal sides
to the new vault. Then to make all the bays of the same scale, the west
bay was also subdivided, but this necessarily at the clerestory level, and
covered with a six-part vault. This left nine bays for the chevet and as
only seven were to be actually included beneath the radiants, a narrow
rectangular four-part vault was used over that toward the choir. There

[31] It may be noted that La Madeleine also resembles St. Germer in having a groined
triforium.

now remained an apse in all respects like those of Saint Martin-des-Champs and of Saint Germain-des-Pres and it was similarly vaulted with a broken-ribbed vault whose keystone does not lie quite upon the transverse line between the first two piers of the apse proper. The chevet built upon these radiants differs, however, from those in Paris and at Saint Germer in having a decidedly domed up character. In other words, the windows do not rise more than half the distance from the impost of the radiants to their keystone.[32]

BUTTRESSING-RIBBED CHEVETS

This type of chevet as developed at Paris and Vezelay played a large part in subsequent architecture, for out of it would seem to have sprung what will be for convenience termed the buttressing-ribbed chevet. Among the more important early chevets of this type are those over the apses of Noyon[33] transepts, of Saint Remi at Reims (Fig. 64), of Saint Leu d'Esse-rent (Oise), and of the cathedrals of Sens, Canterbury, Noyon, and others, all probably completed before 1180. Although differing in a number of details, these apses have certain features in common. They all include beneath the chevet the preceding bay of the church, and all have the same arrangement of ribs which are so placed that the two springing from the piers next beyond the apsidal arch on either side form a transverse arch against whose crown all the others abut (Plate II-d). The object of this arrangement evidently lay in the desire of the builders to construct a dis-tinct transverse arch between the curve of the apse and the rectangular bay included in the chevet and at the same time to employ the two ribs beyond those forming the arch, as buttresses, to offset the thrust of the remaining radiants. Thus when the rectangular bay was larger than those around the curve, as for example in the choir of Soissons cathedral (Fig. 67), the buttressing ribs were longer than the remainder of those forming the vault. This made the bay containing these two ribs precisely like one-half of a six-part vault, and as this method of vaulting was commonly used in the nave and choir of these churches this chevet was a very

---

[32] Vaults with just such doming were to be used side by side with those with higher window cells, as is later shown.

[33] Unfortunately the vaults of Sens and Noyon have been rebuilt though apparently' in the original manner, while those of Senlis, which would have been of much value, have been reconstructed in a later style.

logical continuation of such a vault. But the builders do not seem to have realized immediately the aesthetic advantage in so planning their churches that such chevet vaults should come next to a six-part vault. At Sens (Fig. 28), however, the perfected use of this new chevet is shown for it is placed directly beyond a six-part bay and its two buttressing ribs are the counterparts of the two diagonals of the sexpartite vault. Once the ad-

FIG. 67.—SOISSONS, CATHEDRAL.

vantage of such an arrangement was grasped, the churches were in many cases planned to provide for an even number of six-part bays in the choir followed by a chevet which carries the same system into the apse of the church. Thus in the cathedrals of Paris and Bourges, and probably originally in that of Soissons, as well as in other churches with six-part vaulting, this chevet became the standard form of eastern termination and the bay preceding the apse was made sexpartite so that the completed church would be uniform throughout.[34] Moreover the apsidal bays of the later chevets,

[34] Examples include: Bologna, San Francesco; Auxerre Cath. (planned for six-part type of vaults), etc.

as for example that at Soissons (Fig. 67) were frequently so planned that the radiants from the piers next beyond the ribs forming the transverse arch containing the keystone, were exact extensions of the buttressing ribs. In other words, except for the subdivision of the eastern bay into three window cells, the chevet corresponded to a true six-part vault inscribed in the space formed by the last bay of the choir and the polygonal-sided apse.

Notwithstanding the fact that the buttressing-ribbed chevet was primarily suited to churches with six-part vaulting, it was by no means confined to these for it is found in a large number which were from the beginning planned for four-part vaults. Among these is the cathedral of Rouen, in which the chevet is of distinctly six-part type with a full-sized choir bay included beneath the vault,[35] and the cathedral of Reims in which all the bays of the chevet are of practically the same size, as in the early churches which gave rise to this form of apse vault. Reims is thus an example of the perseverance of the design of a seven-sided chevet including one bay with parallel walls and yet of the same size as those forming the curve.[36]

But while pleasing in appearance when used in combination with six-part choir vaults, the chevet with buttressing ribs was not so satisfactory in churches with four-part cross-ribbed vaulting of rectangular plan. A reference to the vault of Soissons cathedral (Fig. 67)[37] will illustrate the faults of such a combination. These lie largely in the three-part vaulted bay. In the first place, though its window cells are practically the same width as those in the remainder of the choir, their crown lines run out at an awkward angle,[38] instead of being practically perpendicular to the outer walls as in the remaining bays of the apse and all those of four-part type. Secondly, the great, triangular, transverse severy is much larger than any of the others in the church and is thus unpleasing when contrasted with them, besides being more difficult to construct because of its larger size. It is not surprising to find, therefore, that a fourth form of chevet was developed and used extensively in churches with four-part vaulting. This

[35] Other examples not mentioned include Albi (Tarn) cath.; Troyes (Aube) cath.; Semur-en-Auxois (Côte-d'or), Notre Dame.

[36] It is possible that it owes this arrangement to the church of Saint Remi (Fig. 64).

[37] Although not originally planned for four-part vaults in the choir, its present arrangement illustrates the combination referred to.

[38] This is not a noticeable fault with sexpartite choir vaulting since the crowns of all the window cells form similar angles.

chevet, which will be termed diagonal-ribbed, is perhaps the most important distinct type developed in Gothic architecture.

DIAGONAL-RIBBED CHEVETS

It has already been noted that there were a number of early apses covered with an elementary kind of chevet which was formed by the use of two diagonal ribs over the semicircle of the apse in exactly the same manner as similar ribs were used in rectangular four-part vaulting. Such a vault as this may have been the prototype of the slightly more developed form to be seen in the radiating chapels of the cathedral of Noyon (before 1167)[39] and in the chapel at the end of one aisle of Notre Dame at Étampes

FIG. 68.—CHARTRES, CATHEDRAL.

(Seine-et-Oise) (cir. 1160). This latter has one extra rib added in what would have been the eastern bay of such a four-part apse vault subdividing it into two window cells and thus producing a four-celled chevet[40] (Plate II-e). It is exactly this principle, applied on a larger scale and with a further subdivision of this outer bay, which may be seen in such chevets as those of Chartres cathedral (Fig. 68) and Saint Étienne at Caen (first quar-

[39] Porter, II, p. 83, Fig. 176.
[40] In referring to chevet vaults, the terms three-celled, four-celled, etc., refer to the number of window panels or severies, while the terms four-part, five-part, etc., refer to the total number of severies in the vault, generally one more than the number of window cells.

ter of thirteenth century) (Fig. 70).[41] Of these, the one at Chartres has the more primitive character, for all of its seven bays are on the curve of a semicircle and thus none of the choir proper is included beneath the chevet (Plate II-f). As a result of this increased number of bays, the intersection of the two diagonal ribs which form the first two radiants on each side, lies at a point comparatively near the keystone of the apsidal arch. This gives a certain uniformity to the size and character of the bays, but the vault is not yet perfect, for the ribs are still noticeably different in length, and more important than this the crowns of the window cells are at an awkward angle with the exterior wall. These faults are, however, much less marked in Saint Étienne, where the apse is greater than a semicircle—though even this chevet is not of the perfected diagonal-ribbed type, since it has no wall ribs and, moreover, is used over an apse of semicircular instead of polygonal plan like those of the developed Gothic period. An example of the perfected vault may be seen, however, above the apse of Amiens cathedral (Fig. 69). Here there are but five bays of the chevet along the curve of the apse proper, the remaining two being continuations of the choir walls (Plate II-g). The diagonal ribs which determine the position of the keystone are therefore precisely such ribs as those in the remainder of the chevet except that the bay in which they lie is of smaller size than those preceding it and thus forms a gradual transition to the still smaller bays comprising the apse proper. As a result of this arrangement of ribs at Amiens, the keystone of the vault is so placed that it not only renders all the radiants of practically equal length but also makes the crown lines of each window cell so nearly perpendicular to the wall as to give a most symmetrical effect to the entire vault. Such a chevet constitutes the finest method of apse vaulting developed in Gothic architecture and in fact may well be considered the most perfect type conceivable, at least from the point of view of appearance. It loses a little in structural character through the fact that the first ribs do not abut the four eastern radiants at as firm an angle as in the previous chevet type,[42] but the advantage gained in the more symmetrical character of the vaulting severies makes up in large degree for this possible fault.

[41] See also the five-part chevet in the cathedral of Saint Louis at Blois (Loire-et-Cher) which is, however, of much later date.

[42] This may explain the fact that the buttressing rib type of chevet persisted side by side with this fourth form.

Chevets with Added Ribs

Nevertheless it may have been a feeling on the part of the builders that there was a lack of abutment to the west of the keystone which led to the introduction of one or more short ribs at this point in a number of

Fig. 69.—Amiens, Cathedral.

chevets of various dates throughout the Gothic era. Thus in the apse of Saint Étienne at Caen (Fig. 70),[43] of Saint Trophime at Arles, and of the cathedral of Notre Dame at Mantes, a single rib runs out from the keystone of the chevet to that of the apsidal arch. (Plate II-h). Nor was this rib a continuation of a ridge rib in the choir, for in the instances just cited no such rib was employed. One is to be seen in a number of churches, among them such widely separated examples as San Saturnino at Pamp-

---

[43] In St. Étienne this rib would seem to be an addition to the original chevet.

lona,[44] Westminster Abbey,[45] and Saint Alpin at Chalons-sur-Marne,[46] All of these churches have diagonal-ribbed chevets, but there are instances of a short rib running to the apsidal arch even where the vault is of the buttressing ribbed type, as for example in the cathedral of Barcelona,[47] where it would seem to have been used to subdivide the great triangular

FIG. 70.—CAEN, SAINT ÉTIENNE.

transverse cell of the vault even more than to provide further apparent abutment for the other radiants (Plate II-i). Even in chevets of the first type with ribs radiating from the keystone of the apsidal arch, a rib is occasionally added in the bay preceding this vault, as for example in Saint Pierre-le-Guillard at Bourges (fifteenth century vaulting), where this short rib runs out only to the crown of the six-part vault with which the last bay of the choir is covered (Plate II-j). Occasionally, too, a church like the cathedral of Moulins (Allier) (1468-1508), with a ridge rib the length of the choir, is terminated by a chevet with radiating ribs which thus receive apparent abutment at their keystone (Plate II-k).

[44] Street, pl. XXV. op. p. 408.

[45] Bond, p. 63.

[46] This church has a rather exceptional chevet in that it is considerably more than a semicircle in plan.

[47] Plan in Street, pl. XVI, opp. p. 306.

A similar purpose of providing apparent abutment would seem to account for the unusual form of the chevets of Bayeux cathedral (thirteenth century), and Sant' Antonio at Padua (after 1232) in which all the radiants which ordinarily stop at the keystone are carried through against the face of the apsidal arch. At Bayeux there are two such ribs (Plate II-l)[48] and at Padua, three (Plate II-m). The latter is also exceptionally interesting in the form of its chevet which is really a combination of the diagonal and the buttressing ribbed type.

Although there are occasional instances like the one at Barcelona, in which the transverse severy of a buttressing ribbed chevet is subdivided only by a ridge rib, it is far more common to find a more extensive subdivision of this bay when such subdivision was undertaken at all. Moreover, it is an interesting fact that many of the elaborated chevet vaults—for it may be noted here that the apse vault was elaborated just as were those in the remainder of the church edifice—are fundamentally based upon the simple chevet with buttressing ribs.

Of these vaults with added ribs, perhaps the simplest are those in which the western bay is subdivided by the introduction of a ridge rib running about half way to the crown of the apsidal arch and there met by two tiercerons rising from the imposts of this same arch (Plate II-n). A good example appears in the cathedral of Bayonne (Basses-Pyrénées) (after 1213), and another in that of Saint Quentin (Aisne) (commenced 1257), while the same subdivision of this severy in combination with other subdivided cells is to be seen in the Marien-kirche at Stargarde (Germany) (fourteenth century) (Plate IV-d).

A second and unusual division of this severy appears in the cathedral of Saint Jean at Perpignan (Pyrénées-Orientales) (1324-1509),[49] where the customary three-part bay containing the buttressing ribs also contains two diagonals precisely like those in a four-part vault (Plate II-o). A similar arrangement, with the addition of a ridge rib (Plate II-p), may be seen in the church of Saint Jean at Ambert (Puy-de-Dôme) (fifteenth and sixteenth centuries). Such subdivisions as these last two quite evidently had for their object not merely a reduction in the size of the spaces

---

[48] The double apse of the Chapel of the Seminaire at Bayeux (thirteenth century) (Baudot and Perrault-Dabot, II, pl. 44) has two chevets of similar character.

[49] Plan in Caumont, p. 590.

to be vaulted but also an effort to retain the buttressing-ribbed type of chevet and still obtain a window cell which would not have the warped surface characteristic of this form.

A still more elaborate subdivision of the rectangular vaulting bay appears in the chevet of Notre Dame-de-l'Épine near Chalons-sur-Marne (1419-1459) (Fig. 71), where this bay contains no diagonals at all but is

FIG. 71.—CHALONS-SUR-MARNE (NEAR), NOTRE DAME-DE-L'ÉPINE.

divided by a series of tiercerons and short ridge ribs in a manner best understood from the plan (Plate II-q). But it is the subdivision of the window cells of the apse proper which is of especial interest at l'Épine, for the method here employed was very widely extended in the later Gothic period. It consists in the introduction into each of these cells of a short ridge rib running from the central keystone to a point about half way to the window crowns where it is met by two tiercerons which rise from the impost of the principal ribs of the chevet on either side of the window. The apparent object of the system is to so subdivide the vault surface as to break up its compound or ploughshare curves and substitute smaller panels whose surfaces are simpler to construct exactly as in the similar nave vaults previously described. This purpose does not show to advantage at l'Épine, where the awkward adjustment between the vault panels and the window heads would seem to indicate that the apse was originally designed for a simple form of chevet with no added ribs. Better examples could be cited, among them Saint Severin at Paris. Such an arrangement of window cells as that in these vaults practically converts the chevet into a ribbed half dome pierced with lunettes which do not rise to its crown. This may clearly be seen from a study of the apse of Saint Jacques at Antwerp (probably sixteenth century), where the vault is unusual in the omission of all the true radiating ribs (Plate II-r). As a matter of fact such ribs were no longer of value since they did not mark the intersection of two vault panels but merely lay along a surface which is almost precisely like a section of a half dome. The tiercerons are still important since they mark the intersection of the window lunettes and carry the weight of the vault down to the piers. They are therefore retained. Thus, while the absence of radiants in Saint Jacques might seem to make this vault structurally less correct than that of l'Épine in reality such is not the case.

Once it became the custom to introduce extra ribs into the chevet, this portion of the church underwent the same treatment as the vault of the nave or choir. Thus in England, to cite only extreme cases of elaboration, the later Gothic produced such vaults as those of Tewkesbury Abbey (between 1325 and 1350),[50] in France, such pendant types as that of Saint Pierre at Caen (probably early sixteenth century), and in Germany such a choir and apse as that of Freiburg cathedral (late fifteenth century) (Fig. 72).[51] The last named is especially interesting as showing the low point reached in rib vaulting for its ribs have almost no function as supporting members, some of them being actually free from the vault panels and are merely used to form a decorative pattern upon a vault which would stand equally well were they entirely removed. Such chevets are, in many cases, clever examples of stone cutting and decorative design but they are lacking in fundamental structural character.

[50] See the illustration in Bond, p. 165.
[51] See also Pirna, Hauptkirche (1502-1546), Hartung, I, pl. 57.

The Number of Chevet Cells

Thus far the discussion of chevets has been distinctly from a structural point of view, but there remain certain other differences between these vaults which are worthy of remark. In the first place, there is the matter of the number of cells comprised in the chevet. The standard during the

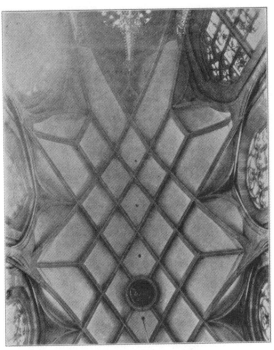

Fig. 72.—Freiburg, Cathedral.

best Gothic period was seven, though five was a frequent number and quite often nine are found (Plate II-s), as for example, in the apse of San Francesco at Bologna, Saint Martin at Ypres, Belgium, and that of Béziers (Hérault), cathedral (1215-1300).[52] In the smaller churches and in the radiating chapels there are frequently three. Moreover, when the apse has a central pier,[53] there are an even number of bays and thus four and six-celled chevets are employed. That in Saint Pierre at Caen, for example,

[52] See also Le Mans, Notre Dame-de-la-Couture; Padua, Sant' Antonio.
[53] And sometimes in churches where this arrangement is not found.

has four bays all on the curve, and that in Notre Dame at Caudebec-en-Caux (Seine-Inférieure) (fifteenth and sixteenth centuries) (Plate II-t) has only two bays thus placed, a fact which gives an angular character to the apse which is far from pleasing.[54] As for the chevets with six cells, they are of very infrequent occurrence, though one is to be seen in Saint Pierre at Auxerre (Plate II-u). A chevet with the unusual number of eleven cells is to be seen in the church of La Chapelle-sur-Crécy (thirteenth century).[55] In construction, this chevet is similar to one bay of such an eight-part vault as that at Provins, Saint Quiriace[56] with its easternmost cell divided into five parts.

The Use of A Central Pier in the Apse

An interesting question arises in this connection as to why the central pier was employed in the mediaeval church. It is not common, yet it occurs frequently enough and over a sufficient space of time to prove that it did not lack a certain amount of popularity. Thus an apse with such a pier is to be seen in the early Romanesque church of Vignory (Haute-Marne) (consecrated cir. 1050-1052), where it is covered by a half dome, and again at Morienval (Oise) (Fig. 77), where there are ribs beneath a similar vault.[57] Throughout the Gothic period, this plan of apse surmounted by a chevet occurs in an even larger number of examples and toward the close of the period becomes quite popular. Leaving out of consideration the origin of the employment of a central eastern pier, which would seem most difficult to ascertain, it is at least interesting to note the effect which a chevet with a central rib presents when compared with the more usual type. If, for example, the apse of Saint Pierre at Auxerre be compared with that of the cathedral of Reims, the advantage and disadvantage of the two methods from the point of view of appearance may be seen. The most displeasing feature of the apse of Reims lies in the fact that its central arch and window, being seen in their full width, seem disproportionately wide in comparison with those on either side, while at Auxerre there is no window shown in its full width with the result that the transition is apparently more gradual from the ends to the center of the apse.

---

[54] See also Neubourg (Eure). Plan in Enlart, I, Fig. 317.
[55] Baudot and Perrault-Dabot, I, pl. 46.
[56] See Fig. 31.
[57] The vault has been recently reconstructed along original lines.

On the other hand, the apse of Reims permits the addition of a lady chapel with an arch on the major axis of the church.[58] Altogether it is largely a question of personal preference which would seem to have guided the builders, combined, perhaps, with some considerations based upon the size of the apsidal curve and as to how many divisions would give the most pleasing form to the apsidal arches. As far as the actual construction of the chevet is concerned, the plan with a central pier made no essential difference, except possibly in the vaulting of the ambulatory which is discussed in the next chapter.

Impost Levels of Chevet Vault Ribs

Another interesting, though minor feature of chevet vaulting, lies in the form of the masonry panels and the position of the imposts of the radiating ribs. The position of the latter varies considerably, though it corresponds in general with the impost level of the transverse arches in the nave or choir of the church. In the best period this was generally somewhat above the sill line of the clerestory windows, but in some of the early churches like Saint Germer (Fig. 63), Saint Quiriace at Provins (Fig. 31), and the cathedral of Bourges (Fig. 76), it is below this line, while in a number of later churches, among them Saint Urbain at Troyes (Aube) (1262-1329) (Fig. 73), it is as high as that of the arches forming the window heads. This last chevet is also important as showing a tendency to do away with the flat wall forming the lower portion of each panel and starting the outward curve of the masonry directly from the extrados of the ribs. Although this detracts somewhat from the beauty of the vault by making the curve of its cells too abrupt, it does prevent large portions of the windows from being concealed and therefore gives a more uniform effect to the clerestory.[59] Such an arrangement of the window cells is to be found even earlier in the chevet of Bayeux cathedral (early thirteenth century), where the rib rises from the clerestory string-course but is kept close against the wall to the impost of the window arches so that the effect produced is much like that at Saint Urbain.

---

[58] A feature which certainly enhances the present appearance of the cathedral, though it is quite possible that the builders originally intended to shut off this vista by a high reredos behind the altar.

[59] Compare for example the chevet of Reims with that of Saint Urbain.

The Shape of the Chevet Cells

Another feature of chevet vaulting which varies greatly throughout its history, is the comparative height of the crown of the wall rib, or line of intersection, and that of the main keystone in other words, of the doming up of the vault panels. In this, there is a very wide divergence all through

FIG. 73.—TROYES, SAINT URBAIN.

the Transitional and Gothic periods. Thus among the early chevets it will be noted that in some the doming is slight though noticeable, as at Saint Germer (Fig. 63), in others it is very pronounced, as at Vézelay (Fig. 66), while in others the crown of the cells actually curves downward toward the central keystone. This is an exceptional type, of which there is an example in Saint Remi at Reims (Fig. 64). Naturally enough, the vault which is most highly domed up exerts the least outward thrust and is thus most easily supported. It is not surprising, therefore, to find this form a favorite where large windows were not required in the apse or where there was no ambulatory or but a low one. This may perhaps explain its use in the south of France in the cathedral of Béziers (Hérault), as well as its popularity throughout Italy, where it may be seen on an exceptionally large scale in the cathedral of Milan. Certain of these domed

FIG. 74.—ANGERS, CATHEDRAL.

up chevets may also be attributed to the type of nave vault developed in the locality in which they are found, as, for example, the chevet of Angers cathedral (Fig. 74), which is very highly domed, with the small torus ribs of the region forming the radiants beneath it. As a matter of fact, such a chevet as this differs from a ribbed-lobed-dome only in having its masonry courses running at right angles to the supporting walls. Its pressures are almost all downward with but little outward thrust though the arrangement of the masonry courses and the shape of the vault cells serves to concentrate both thrusts and pressures upon the ribs and piers instead of along the whole curve of the outer walls, thus rendering perfectly safe the introduction of large windows.[60]

Chevets with Pierced Panels

Still another interesting characteristic of certain chevet vaults is the presence of openings from one cell to the next in the lower portion of the

FIG. 75.—AUXERRE, CATHEDRAL.

panels between them. The simplest of these are to be seen in the cathedral of Auxerre (choir finished 1234) (Fig. 75), and it seems very reasonable from their square shape, comparatively small size, and their position at the beginning of the curve of the vault cells to assume that they were intended to hold wooden beams, used, quite possibly, as supports for scaffolding or centering for the rest of the vault. Whatever their use, they may be the prototypes of such larger openings as those in the cathedral of Bourges (after 1215) (Fig. 76), which may not only have been used

[60] Needless to say, no flying-buttresses are necessary with such a vault as the thrusts are easily absorbed by the piers.

in a similar manner but which, from their circular shape and moulded
character, supply a certain amount of decoration to this part of the vault
and even serve in a slight degree to distribute the light from its windows
over a larger area.[61] An even greater amount of decoration is obtained by
the use of tracery in the similar openings in the cathedral of Orleans
(begun 1630), which are of larger size and of a generally triangular

FIG. 76.—BOURGES, CATHEDRAL.

shape.[62] The final development of such tracery panels may be seen in the
Brunnenkapelle of Magdeburg cathedral (fourteenth century)[63] where
the apse vault proper becomes practically a flat ceiling the entire space between it and each of the ribs being filled with tracery.

[61] Similar openings are to be seen in the apse of Saint Nazaire at Carcassonne.
[62] For other examples showing the employment of this feature even in the Renaissance
see Enlart, I, p. 506, note 2.
[63] Hartung, I, pl. 15.

CHAPTER IV

AMBULATORY VAULTS

Early Ambulatories

It is not the province of this essay to enter into a discussion of the origin of the ambulatory and its introduction into the church plan.[1] It is sufficient to note that a passage around a semicircular apse appears even in Roman times in the imperial tribune of the so-called stadium of Domitian on the Palatine at Rome which dates from the second century A.D.,[2] and that a similar passage was added around the apse of San Giovanni in Laterano by Pope Sergius II (844-845).[3]

Such ambulatories were mere service galleries, not directly connected with the apse and in fact shut off from it by a solid wall, but when once adopted as a feature of the church plan, the ambulatory rapidly became an aisle around the apse corresponding in all respects to that which flanked the rectangular nave or choir.[4] It was·natural, therefore, that this added aisle should have been vaulted and such is the case in the two earliest ambulatories of any size which still exist, namely, those in Santo Stefano at Verona (end of tenth century) and the cathedral of Ivrea (973-1001 or 1002),[5] while the early ambulatories in France, like those of Saint Martin at Tours (end of eleventh century) and the cathedral of Clermont-Ferrand, which have unfortunately been destroyed, were doubtless also vaulted.

---

[1] For a discussion of this point see E. Gall's series of articles on the ambulatory in Monatschefte fur Kunstwissenschaft, beginning with the fifth volume, 1912, pp. 134-149.

[2] See Rivoira I, p. 184.

[3] Now destroyed. See Rivoira I, p. 184.

[4] Some examples of the walled off ambulatory are found, however. See Enlart, I, p. 234, note 5.

[5] See Rivoira, I, p. 183, for dates of Santo Stefano and Ivrea.

Origin of Ambulatory Vaulting

That the form which such vaulting assumes owes its origin to that of the concentric aisles in earlier buildings of circular plan would seem a most natural supposition since the problems in the two cases were precisely alike. As a matter of fact, a comparison shows that all or nearly all the methods of vaulting developed in the Roman or Byzantine period for the aisles of circular buildings were tried by the Romanesque builders when they added an ambulatory to the semicircular apses of their churches.

Annular Tunnel Vaults

The principal Roman type would seem to have been the annular tunnel vault. An excellent example is to be seen in the amphitheatre at Nîmes in which the builders have even employed transverse arches of stone beneath the vault of brick.[6] Similar in character, though later in date and without transverse arches, is the fourth century annular vault of Santa Costanza in Rome. It is not surprising, therefore, to find the annular tunnel vault in a number of the earliest Romanesque ambulatories as, for example, at Ivrea and in the lower story of Santo Stefano at Verona, both dating from the close of the tenth century, and somewhat later at Vignory in France and in the gallery of the Tower chapel in London.[7] The annular tunnel vault never became in any sense a popular form, however, probably because it necessitated an impost above the level of the apsidal arches and exerted a continuous thrust throughout its whole extent. It is more often to be found in crypts, as in Saint Wipertus near Quedlinburg (936)[8] and in Chartres cathedral (1020-1028)[9] where there were no structural problems of support, or else with its imposts lowered and cut by lunettes into an interpenetrating form which is really an elementary groined vault and is later discussed.

[6] An annular tunnel vault also covered the passage around the tribune of the so-called stadium of Domitian already mentioned. See Rivoira, I, p. 184.

[7] For other examples, see Enlart, I, p. 266, note 6. A similar vault is sometimes found in the aisles of circular churches, as for example in Ste. Croix at Quimperlé (eleventh century). Baudot and Perrault-Dabot, II, pl. 5.

[8] See Rivoira, II, p. 289.

[9] At intervals this vault is cut by lunettes or groined bays but it is fundamentally an annular tunnel vault.

AMBULATORIES WITH HALF TUNNEL VAULTS

Besides these annular vaults, there are a few examples of ambulatories with half tunnel vaults which may owe their origin to the desire of the builders to keep the outer impost of the vaults as low as possible and still raise the inner line above the apsidal arcade.[10] In any event such an ambulatory is occasionally found in churches where the aisles also are half-tunneled, as, for example, in the abbey church of Montmajour (cir. 1015-1018)[11] and in the twelfth century church of Saintes.[12] Though this type of vault apparently has no pre-Romanesque prototype, it is perhaps possible that the concentric aisle of the circular church of Rieux-Merinville (Aude) (eleventh century)[13] affords an earlier example of its use over a space of similar plan. There is also an interesting use of a half-tunnel vaulted triforium above the ambulatory and abutting the half dome of the apse which opens into it through five arches, in the church of Loctudy (Finistère) twelfth century.[14]

There are, however, circular buildings of the Byzantine and Carolingian periods with vaulted aisles which may well have furnished the prototypes for other methods of ambulatory vaulting which the Romanesque builders employed. One of these is the Royal Chapel at Aachen (796-804), in which the aisles are two stories high with the lower story covered by groined vaults of alternately square and rectangular plan with no transverse arches separating the bays.[15]

ROMANESQUE AMBULATORIES WITH ALTERNATING TRIANGULAR AND SQUARE BAYS

Although there appear to be no Romanesque churches with ambulatories of exactly this type, there are a number which are composed of triangular sections of an annular vault alternating with groined bays of practically square plan. One of these is the upper ambulatory of Santo Stefano (end of tenth century) at Verona, while a similar arrangement

---

[10] Exactly as has been suggested in regard to similar side aisle vaults.
[11] See Enlart, I, p. 266, note 6.
[12] Enlart, I, p. 34, Fig. 14.
[13] Revoil, I, pl. XLVIII.
[14] Baudot and Perrault-Dabot, II, pl. 25.
[15] Rivoira, II, p. 270, Fig. 718.

may be seen in the concentric aisle of the crypt of Saint Benigne at Dijon (Côte d'Or) (1002-1018).[16] Moreover, the type at Aachen of alternate square and triangular groined bays, is to be seen at Paris with the addition of transverse arches between the bays, in Saint Martin des Champs (cir. 1136) and at Gloucester in the beautiful ambulatory of the cathedral (1089-1100). Furthermore, this alternation of square and triangular bays was of quite frequent occurrence in the ribbed vaulted ambulatories later described.

AMBULATORIES WITH TRANSVERSE TUNNEL VAULTS

The gallery of the Palatine chapel at Aachen is covered in still another manner by a series of ramping tunnel vaults alternately triangular and square in plan and springing from a series of transverse arches. Although never exactly copied in ambulatory vaulting, a similar system in which ramping groined vaults displace the simple tunnel form appears in the gallery of the north transept of San Fedele at Como (twelfth century)[17] while the system of ramping the vault had still another application in the trapezoidal groined vaults of San Tommaso at Almeno-San-Salvatore,[18] the evident object being to get a slant above the vaults suitable for an exterior roof which might rest directly upon them. But if ramping tunnel vaults were not used over the ambulatory, there are at least two instances of the employment of expanding transverse tunnel vaults in this position and these may well be products of the Aachen type. The ambulatory at Vertheuil[19] affords an example dating from about the middle of the twelfth century, which must soon have been followed by the gallery of the cathedral of Notre Dame at Mantes (beg. in 1160?)[20] Here the vaults are similar, but on a much larger scale, and with quite different transverse supports consisting of lintels, each resting upon two columns placed between the apsidal piers and the outer walls.[21]

---

[16] See Rivoira, II, p. 8. See also the Duomo Vecchio at Brescia (Porter, Cons. of Lombard and Gothic Vaults, Fig. 49).

[17] Porter, Cons. of Lombard and Gothic Vaults, Fig. 53.

[18] Porter, Cons. of Lombard and Gothic Vaults, Fig. 52.

[19] Enlart, I, p. 273, Fig. 105.

[20] The date of this cathedral is uncertain and the exceptional character of its triforium leads to the suspicion that it may not now retain its original arrangement, though the writer has no proof of this suggestion.

[21] In some instances these lintels have been cut through with an arch running up into the surface of the vault between the bays.

AMBULATORIES WITH GROINED VAULTED TRAPEZOIDAL BAYS

All of the ambulatory types thus far described were but occasionally used in the Romanesque period. Far more common, and in fact the standard form, is that of simple four-part groined vaults over bays of trapezoidal plan. Here again the plan at least has a Byzantine prototype in the church of San Vitale at Ravenna where the concentric aisle is divided into trapezoids, though these in turn are cut by the radiating niches of the central nave and the groined vaults employed are therefore of irregular form.

Even without any prototypes, however, this arrangement of bays is a direct outcome of the use of an annular tunnel vault intersected by lunettes or transverse tunnels opposite the apsidal arches. Such vaults may in fact be seen at a comparatively early date in the churches of Bois-Sainte-Marie (Saône-et-Loire) (twelfth century), Champagne (Ardeche), and Preuilly-sur-Claise (Indre-et-Loire), and in a reversed sense at Saint Savin (Vienne) (cir. 1020-1040) where there is an early instance of a simple annular vault cut by expanding transverse tunnel vaults whose intrados at the smaller end corresponds to that of the apsidal arches but whose crowns rise higher than that of the vault which they intersect. There are no transverse arches and yet the vault is really composed of a series of trapezoidal bays. The ambulatory of Saint Sernin at Toulouse (choir consecrated 1096) shows this same system in its fully developed form. There are still no transverse arches, but the vault is no longer interpenetrating but fully groined, yet with practically level crowns, so that it still has the general form of intersecting tunnel vaults.

It was far more common, however, for the Romanesque builders to separate their trapezoidal bays by transverse arches, though their use would seem to have been optional rather than to indicate a more developed architectural type, since they are found at an early date in the ambulatory of Saint Philibert at Tournus (Saône-et-Loire) (1009-1019), where the form of the vault would otherwise be of interpenetrating type. It is, in fact, less developed than that at Saint Sernin, the transverse panels being considerably lower than the concentric portion of the vault thus forming simple lunettes above the window heads. In such a vault, the transverse arches are structurally valuable only in so far as they make possible the erection of the vault in sections and consequently serve as permanent centering and as a stiffening member between the apsidal piers and the outer walls. In the fully developed vaults with transverse arches, like those at Paray-le-Monial these arches serve still another purpose. Here it is evident that the vault was laid up in sections, for each bay is domed up at the crown and the transverse arch not only carries a little of the weight of the vault but also conceals what would otherwise be an awkward intersection line between one bay and the next. With this doming up of the vault crown and the use of pointed transverse arches to replace the awkward stilted form, the vault of Paray-le-Monial marks the highest point possible before the introduction of the diagonal rib in the Transitional and Gothic periods.

Ambulatories with Ribbed Vaults

It has already been stated that it is not the purpose of this paper to discuss the origin of ribbed vaulting. In fact, it is rather the intention to accept the conclusions of Mr. Porter in his "Construction of Lombard and Gothic Vaults" that this innovation arose from the necessity for providing a centering where wood was not to be easily obtained or where the shape of the bays or their position in the church made a permanent centering of stone or brick far superior to, and easier of construction than, a similar centering in wood.[22] Accordingly the fact that some of the earliest ribbed vaults appear over the ambulatory is readily explained by the trapezoidal shape of the vaulting bays, for which a wooden centering would have been especially difficult to construct.

Morienval

Of these rib-vaulted ambulatories, the earliest which has come down to us would seem to be that of the little church of Morienval (Figs. 77, 78, 79), which probably dates from about 1120-1130. A study of this ambulatory shows most clearly the gradual changes and adjustments which mark the development of perfected rib vaulting from its groined prototype. In size this is an insignificant work and yet historically most important. Perhaps its first noticeable feature lies in the use of slightly pointed apsidal arches (Fig. 77), showing that the builders grasped in at least a rudi-

---

[22] Previous to Porter there had been suggestions of this origin of the ribbed vault in Choisy's work and in Rivoira's Lombardic architecture, but their studies had been largely confined to vaults whose ribs were sunken into the masonry panels.

mentary way the advantage to be gained in thus bringing these arches up
to a point where they would be nearly, at least, on a level with the crown of
a semicircular formeret. The use of these formerets or wall arches is a
second advance in this vault at Morienval, and though these are unneces-

FIG. 77.—MORIENVAL, CHURCH.

sarily heavy and in two orders (Fig. 78) they do reduce the width of the
vaulting bays and furthermore they clearly define the wall line of the panels
and may even have aided in the support of the wooden centering or *cerce* on
which the severies were laid up. They do not apparently support the actual
masonry of the cell, which, as is clearly shown in the southwest bay, does
not follow the curve of the formeret.[23] The transverse arches (Fig. 78)
show little structural advance, for they are still round headed. They are
however highly stilted yet in addition to this the builders have found it
necessary to pile their crowns with masonry in the manner already described in connection with the vaults at Bury.[24] It is in the use and ar-

[23] See discussion of this point on p. 136.
[24] See p. 53, 54.

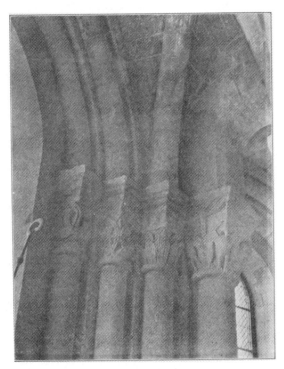

FIG. 78.—MORIENVAL, CHURCH.

FIG. 79.—MORIENVAL, CHURCH.

rangement of the diagonals (Fig. 79) that the chief interest in this early ambulatory lies. If not unknown in bays of rectangular plan, this was probably a first attempt to apply these intersecting ribs to bays of trapezoidal shape, a problem especially difficult when these bays had two curved sides. The ambulatory was so narrow and the wall piers with the two wall arches extended so far into its width that the space actually to be covered was of such a plan that ribs directly from the one pier to that diagonally opposite would have intersected almost against the crown of the apsidal arch. To avoid this awkward arrangement, and make the panels of more equal size, the builders either timidly broke the line of the rib, as in the second bay from the southwest (Fig. 79), or curved the ribs slightly away from the crown of the apse arches as in the northwest bay. Whether the builders were actually experimenting here at Morienval with the position of the diagonals and whether this little work of the early twelfth century had any influence upon later ambulatory vaulting may be an open question, yet it is a fact that the later ambulatories with ribbed vaults over trapezoidal bays show three distinct types in the arrangement of the diagonals according as these are left straight in plan, or curved, or broken to bring their crowns to a better point in relation to the crown line of the enclosing arches.

Trapezoidal Ambulatory Vaults with Straight Diagonal Ribs

Of the three types, the one with straight diagonals (Plate III-a) is perhaps most seldom seen, probably because of the awkward place at which its vault crown falls. It does appear, however, in the cathedral of Aversa near Naples[25], where the heaviness of the ribs would seem to denote an early date.[26] There are a few later examples elsewhere, among

[25] Plan in Rivoira, I, p. 222, Fig. 327.

[26] If Signor Rivoira is correct in his attribution of this ambulatory to the third quarter of the eleventh century (Rivoira, I, pp. 222, 223), it affords not only an extremely early example of the straight ribbed type but an instance of a ribbed vaulted ambulatory of large size antedating that at Morienval by half a century. I am not prepared to accept this early date. The general elevation of the piers and ribs, the geographical situation of the church, the lack of any similarly vaulted ambulatories in the fifty years following its construction and the very form of the vaults, which may easily have once been of the groined type to be seen in the gallery of Santo Stefano at Verona with ribs added at a later date or reconstruction (note lower imposts of diagonal ribs and expanding sofits of transverse arches like those at Verona) together with many other details a discussion of which the limits of this paper forbids, make it seem most improbable that this ambulatory dates from 1049-1078. As a matter of fact, the date is of little importance in the present connection, since it is the type of vault employed with which this study is largely concerned.

PLATE III

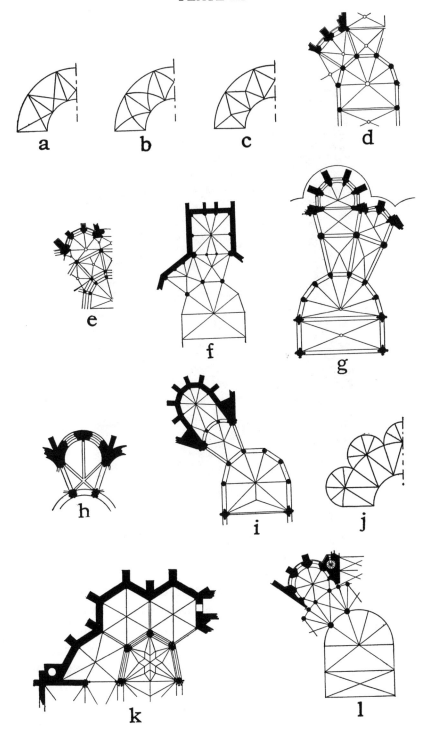

them the cathedrals of Langres (Haute-Marne) (end of twelfth century)
(Fig. 80) and Milan (beg. 1386), while a similar system with one or more
added ribs in the outer severy is to be seen at Pontoise (Seine-et-Oise)

FIG. 80.—LANGRES, CATHEDRAL.

S. Maclou (Plate III-h), in the cathedral of Rouen (Plate III-d), and in
Saint Remi at Reims (Fig. 83), which are later described.

TRAPEZOIDAL AMBULATORY VAULTS WITH CURVED DIAGONAL RIBS

A little more common, perhaps, are the ambulatories with diagonal
ribs of curved plan (Plate III-b). The earliest existing example subsequent to Morienval would seem to be that of the abbey church at Saint
Germer-de-Fly (cir. 1130-1150).[27] Its ribs correspond in general to the
curve of the groins which would be produced by the intersection of a

[27] Plan and interior view in Moore, pp. 72, 73, Figs. 26, 27.

transverse with an annular tunnel vault. Such ribs are naturally difficult to construct because of their curvature in plan as well as in elevation and as a result they are but seldom found, though an example on a large scale appears in Bourges cathedral (Plate IV-a).

TRAPEZOIDAL AMBULATORY VAULTS WITH BROKEN RIBS

The solution of the problem of covering a trapezoidal bay with ribbed vaults lay in the employment of the broken rib, or in other words, in the selection of a point of intersection from which four half arches were extended to the supporting piers (Plate III-c). This system, which was very possibly first employed at Saint Denis (1140-1144),[28] became the standard throughout the best Gothic period wherever trapezoidal bays were used, though there was a certain amount of variance in the position of the keystone. At Saint Denis, and in the great majority of the best Gothic churches it lies practically on the line of a curve through the crowns of the apsidal arches and concentric with that of the apse,[29] but in some instances, notably at Sens cathedral[30] and in the ambulatory of Canterbury[31] which was directly influenced by the first-named church, the point of intersection was moved outward to a point where the line from this crown to the transverse arch is practically perpendicular to the latter. The result is an equalizing in length of the four half ribs, but this is accomplished only at a considerable sacrifice in appearance.[32]

METHOD OF CONSTRUCTION IN AMBULATORY VAULTS

The actual construction of ambulatory vaulting followed much the same course as that of vaults in the remainder of the church and especially those in the side aisles. Thus in the cathedral of Langres (Fig. 80), which dates from the close of the twelfth century and is somewhat south of the center of architectural development in the Transitional period, the ambulatory presents a number of rudimentary characteristics. In fact, judging from the awkward manner in which the diagonals rise from their

---

[28] Plan in Moore, p. 83, Fig. 34.

[29] This may be plainly seen at the cathedral of Tournai (Fig. 85).

[30] Moore, Mediaeval Church Architecture of England, p. 96, Fig. 82 and pl. XV, opp. p. 104.

[31] Crypt illustrated in Moore, Mediaeval Church Architecture of England, p. 94, Fig. 80, Trinity chapel, p. 103 Fig. 86 and pl. XIV. opp. same page.

[32] See Moore, Mediaeval Church Architecture of England, pp. 94-95.

imposts, the exceptionally large size of the transverse arches, and the lowness of those opening into the apse, it would seem as though this aisle had been planned for domed up groined vaulting of the Bourgogne type, already seen at Paray-le-Monial, and that ribbed vaulting came in before the completion of the ambulatory and was therefore substituted. In any event, these straight diagonals and low apsidal arches combined with the heavy transverse arches and the decidedly domed up character of the vaults themselves produce a much more primitive appearance than is to be seen further north in the contemporary vaults of Saint Leu-d'Esserent (Fig. 81). In the latter, the builders have stilted the apsidal and trans-

FIG. 81.—SAINT LEU-D'ESSERENT, ABBEY CHURCH.

verse arches, thus greatly reducing the doming of the vaults. They have also provided an impost for the diagonals which are themselves of the broken type, and in fact the form of the vaults is practically perfected except in the matter of the transverse arches. These are still much heavier than the diagonals, a feature which continues to be manifest though in a less marked degree in many of the ambulatory vaults even of the thirteenth century. They correspond in this respect to side aisle vaulting.[33] Only occasionally, as in the splendid inner ambulatory of Le Mans cathedral (1218-1254), were the ribs all made of the same size. This advance combined with its height and general character may perhaps entitle the ambulatory of Le Mans to rank as the finest in Gothic architecture and the high water mark of the trapezoidal four-part broken ribbed vault.

TRAPEZOIDAL AMBULATORY VAULTS WITH ADDED RIBS

If there was one fault in the broken ribbed type of ambulatory vault just described, it lay in the form of its intersection with the outer wall. For example, if the ambulatory was comparatively low or the apsidal arches of wide span, this intersection became either segmental or semicircular or, at best a very low pointed curve, under which it was most difficult to arrange the exterior windows and still produce a pleasing interior effect. Thus in the ambulatory of Sens cathedral,[34] the two round headed windows do not fill the space beneath the wall rib and are in fact awkwardly placed beneath it, while in the ambulatory of Trinity chapel in Canterbury cathedral,[35] where the vaults are but slightly domed, the arrangement is even less pleasing. Of course when these arches opened into radiating chapels, their shape did not make so much difference since their supporting piers ran all the way to the floor and therefore gave a fairly good proportion to the arch. But if the entire space beneath them were occupied by a window extending only part way to the floor, it would be largely head and very little jamb and thus of displeasing proportions. Even in the ambulatory clerestory of Le Mans, where the transverse and diagonal ribs are all of very pointed section, the window is too broad for its height. It would seem, therefore, to have been with an eye to a more pleasing arrangement of the windows beneath these trapezoidal vaults, that many of the mediaeval builders subdivided the outer severy of extra ribs running out from the central keystone. This made possible two or more windows in the outer wall of each bay. Thus in the alternate bays of the ambulatory of Rouen cathedral (Plate III-d), where there are no radiating chapels, a single rib is added in the outer panel making the vault of five-part form, so that the heads of the two slender windows of the bay are

---

[33] See p. 99 for theory regarding this.

[34] Moore, Mediaeval Church Architecture of England, pl. XV, opp. p. 104.

[35] Moore, Mediaeval Church Architecture of England, pl. XIV, opp. p. 103.

each situated in a separate cell. This same arrangement is characteristic
of a number of other ambulatories, including the lofty inner one at Coutances cathedral (Fig. 82, and Plate III-e),[36] where the windows are

Fig. 82.—Coutances, Cathedral.

limited in height by the elevation and would be of awkward shape were
they not arranged in pairs under separate vault cells.[37] Nor did the
mediaeval builders restrict themselves to a single added rib in this outer

[36] Ambulatories vaulted in a similar manner appear in Saint Sauveur at Bruges, the
Groote Kerk at Breda, the cathedral of Burgos, the church at Gonesse (Seine-et-Oise)
(plan in Enlart, I, p. 486, Fig. 233) etc. Also, in Magdeburg Cath. (Hartung I, pl. 16),
there is an instance in which the intermediate rib is shortened evidently to admit the
greatest possible amount of light.

[37] This is also a church employing the lancet type of window common in Normandy
and England and the subdivision of the ambulatory thus made possible windows of
general lancet shape. Furthermore, it carried the subdivision of the triforium arcade
into the clerestory above. (For a large photograph of this ambulatory see Gurlitt, pl. 84).

severy of the vault. In the ambulatory gallery of Saint Remi at Reims
(Fig. 83) there is an excellent example of the subdivision of this panel

FIG. 83.—REIMS, SAINT REMI.

into three window cells and in the church of Saint Germain and the cathedral at Auxerre (Fig. 84 and Plate III-f) there are excellent examples of
a similar method, applied both in bays with exterior windows and in those
which open into a radiating chapel. In the latter instance, the lofty and
slender shafts between this chapel and the ambulatory with their many
radiating ribs and arches give a charming appearance of grace and lightness to the design.

AMBULATORY VAULTS WHICH INCLUDE THE RADIATING CHAPELS

In all the churches thus far discussed, and, in fact, in the majority of
those constructed during the Gothic period, the radiating chapels are separated from the rest of the ambulatory by arches directly across their en-
trances. But quite frequently these chapels, particularly when they were
comparatively shallow, as in the cathedral of Chartres (Plate III-g), or

even when comparatively deep as at Saint Denis[38] and Saint Maclou at Pontoise (Plate III-h), were treated as part of the ambulatory and an added rib was introduced in vaulting them exactly in the manner described in connection with the trapezoidal bays of Rouen and Coutances. Furthermore, as the chapels were increased in size, more than one extra rib was added in the severy of the trapezoidal vault which embraced them so that

FIG. 84.—AUXERRE, CATHEDRAL.

there were, sometimes, two such ribs, as in the cathedral of Tournai (1240-1260) (Fig. 85).[39] Occasionally, also, as in the cathedral of Saint Quentin (after 1230) (Plate III-i), similar bays and vaults occur, with the addition of large radiating chapels opening off of the more shallow curves of the ambulatory bays, suggesting a combination of the Tournai type with that of Auxerre (Plate III-f). In some of the larger and deeper chapels there were even four added ribs as, for example, in the cathedral

[38] Plan in Moore, p. 83, Fig. 34.
[39] Similar vaults appear at Coutances Cath., outer ambulatory, Utrecht Cath. (ridge ribs added) Malmo, Ch., and Lagny, Ab. Ch. (illustrated in Lenoir, part II, p. 207).

Fig. 85.—Tournai, Cathedral.

Fig. 86.—Bayonne, Cathedral.

of Bayonne (Fig. 86), where the ambulatory is further noteworthy because the builders, in an attempt to equalize the vaulting severies, have moved the keystones of the diagonals almost out to a point on the line of the outer walls. As a matter of fact, it was moved out to such a point in a number of instances (Plate III-j), as, for example, in Soissons cathe-. dral[40] where it becomes the keystone of an arch directly across the entrance of the chapel as well as being the center for all the ribs both of this chapel and the ambulatory. Each trapezoidal bay is thus divided not into four but into three triangular panels, the chapel itself being covered by a fully developed five-part chevet vault for which the two ribs of the ambulatory bay act as buttresses. A similar but more logical vault appears in the ambulatory and two eastern chapels of Pamplona cathedral (begun 1397) (Plate III-k). This is a church with an axial eastern pier, and its radiating chapels are arranged so as to form perfect hexagons with the bays of the ambulatory. The keystone is then moved out, as at Soissons, to the crown of the chapel arch where it lies in the exact center of each hexagonal bay and thus produces a perfectly symmetrical vault.

Ambulatories with Alternate Square and Triangular Bays

Although the trapezoidal bay and its variants has been the only one thus far considered in the discussion of ribbed vaulted ambulatories, it was not by any means universally employed. The alternation of square and triangular bays, which had been used as early as the Carolingian period in the royal chapel at Aachen, and in the tenth century at Verona, in groined vaulted ambulatories, also played a considerable rôle after the use of ribs became general. This system afforded a number of structural advantages, the chief one being, of course, that the major bays were square or nearly so, and therefore presented no structural problems not already solved in other portions of the church, while the triangular divisions were of comparatively small size and could be covered in the same manner as in the Romanesque period, with three-part groined vaults, provided the builders wished to avoid attempting ribbed vaults over them.

Two general plans are noticeable in the use of this alternate ambulatory system. In the first, which appears at an early date in Saint Martin of Étampes (1165), Saint Remi at Reims (1170-1181), and Notre Dame

---

[40] Plan in Enlart, I, p. 505, Fig. 244.

at Chalons-sur-Marne (end of twelfth century), the square bays alternate
with two triangular bays or, in other words, the ambulatory is first divided into trapezoids by transverse arches and these in turn subdivided
into a square and two triangles. This system may be understood from the
plan of Saint Remi (Plate III-1) and the interior view of the same
church (Fig. 87). Its most noticeable feature is the lack of ribs in the

FIG. 87.—REIMS, SAINT REMI.

triangular bays, these remaining of simple Romanesque groined type. Exactly the same arrangement appears at Chalons-sur-Marne, except that
here the arches into the apse correspond to the flat sides of a polygon,
while those opening into the chapels are on a curve in order that the exterior wall of the triforium above them may be a semicircle.[41] In both

[41] Violet-le-Duc (Vol. IV, pp. 75-77) calls attention to the architectural refinements in
this church, mentioning the use of arches flattened on their inner face and curved on
the outer between the apse and triforium. It is also interesting to note that here

these churches, the radiating chapels occupy all the space included beneath each group of three outer arches in a manner similar to that described in connection with the cathedral of Auxerre, but in Saint Martin at Étampes, the chapel is limited in width to the span of the central arch, making possible a window in the exterior wall of each of the triangular bays. A very similar arrangement appears in the outer ambulatory of Bourges cathedral (cir. 1195-1215) (Plate IV-a), except that here the chapels are so narrow as to give a reversed trapezoidal character to what would otherwise be a square bay like that at Étampes and Saint Remi. Even though the triangular severies are thus increased in size, the builders have left their vaults unribbed.

The second system of alternating square and triangular bays may be seen in the outer ambulatory of the cathedral of Le Mans (Plate IV-b) and in both ambulatories of the cathedral at Toledo (1227—seventeenth century).[42] It is the familiar early mediaeval system of a single triangular bay between two squares with the addition of ribs beneath the vaults in all the bays. The chief effect of this system upon the construction was to subdivide the outer line of the ambulatory into twice as many parts as there were in the apse. This created a certain difficulty in the adjustment of the buttresses, for the lack of any transverse arch directly across the ambulatory from the apsidal piers to the outer walls made necessary the subdivision of the flying-buttresses into two parts. This subdivision must have added considerably to the expense and difficulty of construction, though this was somewhat offset by the reduced size of the buttress piers and their position in the thickness of the chapel walls, where they in no way interfered with the introduction of windows directly in the outer walls of the triangular ambulatory bays. Though not extensively employed, this vaulting system which is to be seen at Le Mans shared with all others the tendency of the late Gothic period to add extra ribs to those forming the real framework of the vaults. Such added ribs are to be seen in Saint Willibrord at Wesel and Saint Lorenz at Nürnberg. Similar also to the

as in Saint Remi the vault of the triforium differs from that of the ambulatory proper. The arrangement at Saint Remi has been described, that at Chalons consists of a simple four-part vault of trapezoidal form with outer and inner sides curved.

[42] Examples at Strassburg, Cath., Neubourg (Eure), ch. (irregular type of ch. with central pier and triangular apse. See plan in Enlart, I, p. 590, Fig. 317) and Tewkesbury Abbey (here even the triangular bays open into chapels). See also Cléry (Loiret) (fifteenth century) (plan in Baudot and Perrault-Dabot, III, pl. 60).

PLATE IV

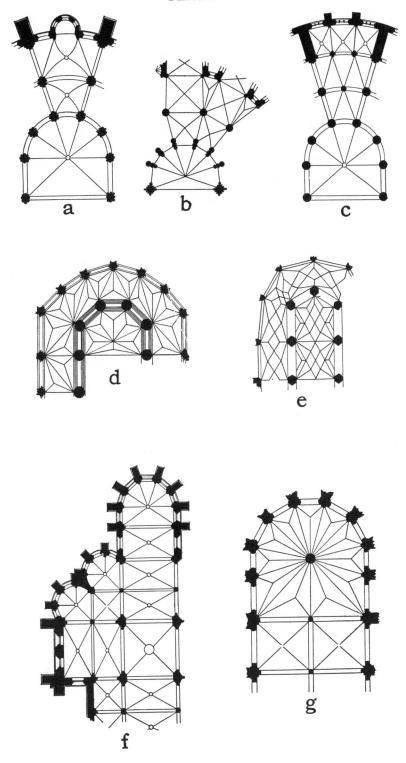

Le Mans type, but with the entire omission of the transverse arches between the triangular and trapezoidal bays, is the system at Saint Pierre-sur-Dives (Calvados)[43] which is thus like the outer ambulatory of Coutances cathedral (Plate III-e), except that the chapels are not included beneath the ambulatory vault and the portions containing the three half ribs are more in proportion to the larger cross ribbed severies.

Ambulatories with Triangular Bays Only

Another method of ambulatory vaulting in the Gothic period consisted in the subdivision of the apsidal aisles into triangles by adding inter-mediate supports between each pier forming the outside corners of trape-zoidal bays. This method, never had a wide popularity. It was used at a comparatively early date and on a large scale in the cathedral of Notre Dame at Paris (begun 1163) (Plate IV-c), where the triangular bays have no ribs beneath their masonry. It appears with the addition of three half ribs or even a still greater number, in a number of late Gothic churches, especially in Germany,[44] and was also used at Saint Eustache (1532-1637)[45] and Saint Severin[46] in Paris, whose builders may very probably have been influenced by the cathedral church of Notre Dame. In Notre Dame, where there are two ambulatories the doubling of the piers did not do away with the possibility of a central eastern chapel or window in the exterior wall. But in most cases, where there is but one aisle, as, for example, in the Marienkirche at Stargarde (end of fourteenth century) (Plate IV-d) or the old cathedral of Heidelberg,[47] an axial pier prevents this arrangement. Perhaps to avoid this the builders of Saint Steven at Nymwegen and of the cathedral at Brandenburg left the eastern bay trapezoidal so that there might be a central Lady chapel. At Kolin[48] where there is an axial pier in the apse a central chapel off the ambu-latory naturally follows.

---

[43] Plan in Caumont, p. 396.

[44] Examples not mentioned include, Beeskow; Keisheim; Stargarde, Johanniskirche (slightly elaborated); Treptow (considerably elaborated); Worms, Liebfrauenkirche; Arles, Saint Trophime, etc.

[45] Plan in Gaudet, III, p. 247, Fig. 1108.

[46] Plan in Gaudet, III, p. 240, Fig. 1104.

[47] These two churches not only show the vault with simple added ribs but the last named is most interesting as showing an ambulatory equal in height to the apse, a most unusual arrangement.

[48] This church also presents certain changes in the arrangement of the ribs but these are unimportant.

Ambulatories with Multiple Ribbed Vaults

As has been noted, the late Gothic passion for multiple ribs affected the ambulatory as it did the remainder of the church, and vaults of most complex character are to be found especially in certain German churches. Of these, Güben (Plate IV-e) and the cathedral of Freiburg (second half of the fifteenth century) (Fig. 88) are among the most elaborate.[49] In them, the structural purpose of the rib is totally subordinated to deco-

Fig. 88.—Freiburg, Cathedral.

rative principles and to a desire on the part of the builders to show their knowledge of the intricate problems of stereotomy. With such vaults as these, marking the decline of Gothic architecture, it is not surprising that there was such a complete reaction in vault construction on the part of the succeeding Renaissance builders.

With this discussion of the ambulatory, the study of mediaeval church

[49] See also Kuttenberg.

vaulting is practically complete, but a few paragraphs should be added to give a short account of some unusual eastern terminations and a brief reference to the radiating chapels. Both of these, while presenting no great structural accomplishments, at least show the skill of the builders in meeting any and all requirements imposed by the plan.

EXCEPTIONAL EASTERN TERMINATIONS

Of the eastern terminations, a number are especially interesting. One is in the church of Saint Yved at Braisne (Aisne) (1180-1216) (Plate IV-f), where there is no ambulatory and yet two chapels have been so arranged with their axes at an angle of forty-five degrees to that of the choir aisle as to form a veritable series of four radiating chapels, two on either side of the principal apse. To cover the triangular bays immediately preceding these chapels, a two-part vault corresponding to one of the diagonal halves of a simple four-part vault, is employed, while the chapel itself is covered with a three-part chevet whose crown is abutted by the half rib of the preceding bay.[50] Occasionally, too, a similar arrangement of chapels is found even where there is an ambulatory as in the church of Saint Nicaise at Reims (now destroyed) and at Upsala. Another termination of interest is that in the church of Vigan (Lot)[51] (fifteenth century) where the apse with its chevet vault is west of the transept, into which it opens through its farthest bay while from the transept itself open five small chapels, a unique arrangement.

A third eastern termination of especial interest is that of the church of the Jacobins at Toulouse (Haute-Garonne) (Fig. 89 and Plate IV-g). Here there is a row of central piers the length of the church and the apse embraces the double nave thus formed. This apse the builders have subdivided into a series of triangular bays by arches springing from a pier at the center of its diameter. Each of these is again subdivided like the triangular ambulatory bays of Le Mans cathedral. This completes a vault

[50] A similar plan on a smaller scale and with only two side chapels occurs at Villeneuve-le-Comte (Seine-et-Marne) (plan in Enlart, I, p. 485, Fig. 232) and the same arrangement in churches with central plan appears at Trier in the Liebfrauenkirche while other examples include Lisseweghe; Toul, Saint Gengoulf; Xant; Oppenheim; Ludinghausen; Anclam; Lubeck, Saint Jakob; Lagny (Seine-et-Marne) (illustrated in Lenoir, Part II, p. 207) and Kaschau (Hungary) (illustrated in Lenoir, Part II, p. 208). See also Enlart, I, p. 485, note 2.

[51] Baudot and Perrault-Dabot, V, pl. 79.

of very beautiful character. It is not, however, an original product in Toulouse, for the crypt of Canterbury cathedral (1175-1184) affords a similar vault of earlier date and others on a circular plan may be seen in a number of English Chapter Houses.

THE VAULTING OF RADIATING CHAPELS

As for the radiating chapels, they were added to the ambulatory with the evident purpose of affording more space for altars especially in the great pilgrimage churches.[52] At the beginning of the eleventh century,

FIG. 89.—TOULOUSE, CHURCH OF THE JACOBINS.

three such chapels had already been built off the ambulatory of Saint Martin at Tours and only slightly later in date are those in La Couture at Le Mans followed by those of a great number of churches of the eleventh and twelfth centuries.[53] Nor are such chapels found only in churches with ambulatories. They frequently open directly off the apse, sometimes being merely recesses in the thickness of the outer wall[54] but more often

[52] Such chapels were frequently omitted all through both the Romanesque and Gothic periods even in churches with an ambulatory and were not therefore established parts of the church plan. For examples of such chapels see Enlart, I, p. 228 note 2 and p. 485 note 3 and Lasteyrie, p. 297.

[53] For discussion of prototypes see Lasteyrie, pp. 187, 188.

[54] For examples see Lasteyrie, p. 301 and Enlart, I, p. 231, note 4.

extending beyond it.[55]   Ordinarily, however, churches with radiating chapels have an ambulatory as well; but even so, there are occasional examples of chapels lying entirely within the thickness of the exterior wall.[56] in which cases they are merely half-domed niches.

Whenever these radiating chapels are found there is considerable variance both in their number and ground plan.   Sometimes there is but one,[57] sometimes two,[58] in the majority of cases three,[59] very seldom four,[60] but frequently five.[61]   In plan, the chapels are generally semicircular with or without one or more preceding rectangular bays.[62]   Naturally they are vaulted exactly in the manner used for the principal apse of the church or the minor apses of the transept at the time the chapels were built.   The usual Romanesque form is the simple half dome like that in Saint Nicolas at Blois, which is especially interesting because it still retains its painted decoration.   As the ribbed half dome came in in apse vaulting it appeared in a number of radiating chapels, at Domont and Saint Martin of Étampes, for example, but the usual Gothic form was the chevet vault which corresponds exactly with that over the major apse, except when it is combined with the ambulatory vault in the manner already described,[63] or is of square,[64] circular, polygonal, or irregular plan.[65]   In such cases the vaulting is adapted to the plan without any great structural changes from the types found in the remainder of the church.   The cathedral of Auxerre (Fig. 84 and Plate III-f), for example, shows the use of a ten-part vault over a square chapel, while Saint Germain also at Auxerre and Saint Remi at Reims (Fig. 87 Plate III-l) have chapels of almost circular plan covered with a vault which is virtually a double Gothic chevet like that of the transept chapels of Soissons and Laon cathedrals already described.[66]

---

[55] For examples see Lasteyrie, p. 301 and Enlart, I, p. 486, note 1.
[56] See Enlart, I, p. 231, note 2.
[57] For examples see Lasteyrie, p. 297, and Enlart I, p. 233, note 1 and p. 486, note 3.
[58] For examples see Lasteyrie, p. 297, and Enlart, I, p. 233, note 2.
[59] For examples see Lasteyrie, p. 297, and Enlart, I, p. 233, note 3.
[60] Orcival (Lasteyrie, p. 297, Fig. 458).
[61] For examples see Enlart, I, p. 233, note 3.
[62] Rather rare in the Romanesque period. For examples see Enlart, I, p. 232.
[63] See page 173 et seq.
[64] For examples of square chapels see Enlart, I, p. 231, note 2 and p. 487, note 7.
[65] For example, the chapels with other chapels added to them toward the east at Norwich cath. and Mehun-sur-Yevre (Cher) see Enlart, I, p. 234, note 4.
[66] See p. 112.

BIBLIOGRAPHY

This bibliography contains in large measure only titles referred to in the text. For further references see bibliography in Porter, Medieval Architecture. The abbreviations listed in the first column are those used in the notes.

Baum	Julius Baum	Romanesque Architecture in France
Baudot and Per-rault-Dabot	A. de Baudot and A. Perrault-Dabot	Archives de la Commission des Monuments Historiques
Bond	Francis Bond	Gothic Architecture in England
Borrmann and Neuwirth	Richard Borrmann und Joseph Neuwirth	Geschichte der Baukunst. 2 vols.
Bumpus	T. Francis Bumpus	A Guide to Gothic Architecture
Butler	Howard Crosby Butler	Abbeys of Scotland
Cattaneo	Raphael Cattaneo	l'Architecture en Italie du VIe au XIe Siecle
Caumont	Arcis de Caumont	Abecedaire ou Rudiment d'Archaeologie
Choisy	Auguste Choisy	Histoire de l'Architecture. 2 vols.
Cummings	Charles A. Cummings	A History of Architecture in Italy. 2 vols.
C. M. H.		Archives de la Commission des Monuments Historique. 1855-72
Dartein	Fernand de Dartein	Etude sur l'Architecture Lombarde et sur les origines de l'Architecture Romano-Byzantine. 2 vols.
Dehio and von Bezold	G. Dehio und G. von Bezold	Die kirchliche Baukunst des Abendlandes. 2 vols., text and 360 plates
Enlart	Camille Enlart	Manuel d'Archaeologie Francaise. 2 vols.
Gosset	Alphonse Gosset	Les Coupoles d'Orient et d'Occident
Gaudet	Julien Guadet	Elements et Theorie de l'Architecture
Gurlitt	Cornelius Gurlitt	Die Baukunst Frankreichs. 8 vols.
Madrazo-Gurlitt	D. Pedro de Madrazo (Spanish text) Cornelius Gurlitt (German text)	Die Baukunst Spaniens
Gwilt	Joseph Gwilt, F.S.A. F.R.S.A.	An Encyclopaedia of Architecture. Revised by Wyatt Angelicus van Sandau Papworth
Hamlin	A. D. F. Hamlin	A Text-book of the History of Architecture
Hartung	Hugo Hartung	Motive der Mittelalterlichen Baukunst in Deutschland
Isabelle	Charles Edouard Isabelle	Les Edifices circulaires et les Domes
Joseph	D. Joseph	Geschichte der Architektur Italiens
Kugler	Franz Theodor Kugler	Geschichte der Baukunst
Lasteyrie	R. de Lasteyrie	l'Architecture Religieuse en France a l'Epoque Romane. Ses origines, son developpement
Lenoir	Albert Lenoir	Architecture Monastique in Collection des Documents inedits sur Histoire de France

185

Lefevre-Pontalis   Eugène Lefevre-Pontalis   l'Architecture Religieuse dans l'Ancien Dio-
cése de Soissons au XIe et au XIIe Siecla

Lubke   Wilhelm Lubke   Outlines of the History of Art. 2 vols. Edited
and revised by Russell Sturgis

M. H.   Archives de la Commission des Monuments
Historique

Michel   André Michel   Histoire de l'Art depuis les premiers temps
Chrétiens jusqu 'á nos jours. Published
under direction of André Michel by a number of collaborators

Moore   Charles Herbert Moore   Development and Character of Gothic Architecture

  Charles Herbert Moore   Mediaeval Church Architecture of England

Mothes   Charles Herbert Moore   Character of Renaissance Architecture

Mothes   Oscar Mothes   Die Baukunst des Mittelalters in Italien

Nesfield   W. Eden Nesfield   Specimens of Mediaval Architecture. Drawings

Osten   Friedrich Osten   Die Bauwerke in der Lombardei vom 7ten bis
zum 14ten Jahrhundert

Porter   Arthur Kingsley Porter   Mediaeval Architecture. Its Origins and
Development. 2 vols.

  Arthur Kingsley Porter   The Construction of Lombard and Gothic
Vaults

Prior   Edward Schröder Prior   The Cathedral Builders in England

Prioux   Stanislas Prioux   Monographie de St. Yved de Braine

Pugin   Augustus Pugin   Specimens of the Architecture of Normandy.
New Edition edited by Richarr Phené Spiers

Ramée   Daniel Ramée   Histoire Générale de l'Architecture. 3 vols.

Reber   Franz von Reber   History of Mediaeval Art

Revoil   Henry Revoil   Architecture du Midi de la France

Rickman   Thomas Rickman   Gothic Architecture, or An Attempt to Discrim-
inate the Styles of Architecture in England
from the Conquest to the Reformation

Rivoira   G. Teresio Rivoira   Lombardie Architecture, translated by G.
McN. Rushforth

Ross   Frederick Ross   The Ruined Abbeys of Britain

Ruprich-Robert   V. Ruprich-Robert   L'Architecture Normande aux XIe et XIIe
Siècles. En Normandie et en Angleterre

Sharpe   Edmund Sharpe   The Seven Periods of English Architecture

Simpson   F. M. Simpson   A History of Architectural Development.
3 vols.

Strange   Edward F. Strange   The Cathedral Church of Worcester. A description of the Fabin and a brief history of
the Episcopal See

Street   Geo. Edmund Street   Gothic Architecture in Spain

Sturgis   Russell Sturgis   A History of Architecture

Uhde   Constantin Uhde   Baudenkmaeler in Grossbrittannien. 2 vols.
Plates

  Constantin Uhde   Baudenkmaeler in Spanien und Portugal

Viollet-de-Duc   Eugène Emmanuel Viol-let-le-Duc   Dictionnaire Raisonne de l'Architecture Fran-
caise du XIe au XVIe Siècle. 10 vols.

Willis   R. Willis   On the construction of the vaults of the
Middle Ages (in the Transactions of the
Royal Institute of British Architects, Vol. I,
Part II).

INDEX

Abbreviations.—Ch., Church; Cath., Cathedral; Ab. Ch., Abbey Church; N. D., Notre Dame; S. M., Santa Maria, Saint Mary, etc.